Where I'm Bound

CONTRIBUTIONS IN AMERICAN STUDIES

Series Editor: Robert H. Walker

Where I'm Bound

Patterns of Slavery and Freedom in Black American Autobiography

Sidonie Smith

CONTRIBUTIONS IN AMERICAN STUDIES

NUMBER 16

Greenwood Press

WESTPORT, CONNECTICUT ● LONDON, ENGLAND

Library of Congress Cataloging in Publication Data

Smith, Sidonie.
    Where I'm bound; patterns of slavery and freedom in
Black American autobiography.

    (Contributions in American studies, no. 16)
    Bibliography: p.
    1. Negroes—Psychology. 2. Negroes—Race identity.
3. Autobiography—History and criticism. I. Title.
E185.625.S64   808   73-20973
ISBN 0-8371-7337-X

(v

Library of Congress Catalog Card Number: 73-20973

ISBN: 0-8371-7337-X

First published in 1974

Greenwood Press, a division of Williamhouse-Regency Inc.
51 Riverside Avenue, Westport, Connecticut 06880

Manufactured in the United States of America

TO

OSCAR and LUCILE SMITH

CONTENTS

PREFACE

The earliest black American autobiographies, the slave narratives, established certain prototypal patterns, both thematic and structural, that recur again and again in subsequent black autobiographies. The ex-slave narrated the story of his successful break *into* a community that allowed authentic self-expression and fulfillment in a social role: his achievement of a "place" within society. He also narrated the story of his radical break *away from* an enslaving community that forbade him authentic selfhood by foisting a false identity upon him: his continual flight to a "place" outside society. This study examines the increasingly complex and ambiguous manifestations of these patterns as they find expression in succeeding generations of autobiographers.

Booker T. Washington's *Up From Slavery* dramatizes the journey of the black self into a place of prominence within American society, a journey reenacted again and again in later black autobiography. In contrast, the life stories of Richard Wright and Langston Hughes explore and finally exhaust the possibility of flight from the oppression of a social identity to a geographical place. The black self is then left without recourse to geographical freedom, and thus, in the contemporary autobiographies to be discussed, the two possibilities have manifested themselves in new ways. The break away from community becomes the recoil from and rejection of white society; the break into a community becomes the acceptance of special black roles within the narrower black community. These alternatives may, however, be a return to imprisonment, not a legitimate means to freedom. For Malcolm X and Eldridge Cleaver, a militant social role becomes a positive possibility, as is Maya Angelou's growth into self-conscious black womanhood. For Horace Cayton and Claude Brown, social roles of any kind are ultimately unsatisfactory. Wright, Cleaver, Angelou, Cayton, and Brown do, however, suggest and dramatize the possibility of another means of escape, one implicit in many slave narratives and the last possibility to be discussed—liberation through the creative act of writing autobiography itself.

The power of these narratives, the self-consciousness of the narrators, the thematic and structural motifs inherent in the works, and their historical significance—all these factors, combined with my own personal preferences, determined their selection. Ultimately, I found it more satisfying to discuss a few autobiographies in detail rather than sacrifice depth for breadth. As a result, certain omissions cry out. W.E.B. DuBois's *Dusk of Dawn* receives only passing reference, James Weldon Johnson's *Along This Way* none at all. In addition to the exclusion of specific works, there are whole areas of black autobiography left undeveloped. The popular tradition—autobiographies of famous personalities, entertainers and athletes—is mentioned only briefly, as is the autobiography of the black woman. My only consolation has been the belief that these traditions deserve books to themselves and that they will soon receive them. Ironically, the sin of omission becomes the best argument for further work on the subject.

I want to thank the Ford Foundation for a grant that allowed me to pursue work undisturbed on the doctoral dissertation from which this book derives; friends, Steve Most, Dave Emmons, Sandy Chrystal, Greg Grieco, Linda Turner, Tim Drescher, for their editorial energies; and Dr. Roger B. Salomon, my dissertation adviser, for his confidence and his integrity as a scholar and teacher.

Where I'm Bound

1

FLIGHT

To be changed from a chattel to a human being, is no light matter. . . . And if I could reach the ears of every slave today, throughout the whole continent of America, I would teach the same lesson, I would sound it in the ears of every hereditary bondman, "break your chains and fly for freedom."
—*Preface to* Narrative of the Life and Adventures of Henry Bibb, An American Slave

On January 1, 1834, a slave named William broke his chains and fled to freedom after twenty-one years in slavery. He had been born in Lexington, Kentucky, slave to Mr. Young, a relative of his white father. Soon after his birth, William's master moved to St. Louis, Missouri, and once the boy was old enough, hired him out to a series of employers, the first of whom was Major Freeland, owner of a public house. This Major Freeland, "in his fits of anger . . . would take up a chair, and throw it at a servant; and in his more rational moments, when he wished to chastise one . . . would tie them up in the smokehouse, and whip them; after which, he would cause a fire to be made of tobacco stems, and smoke them."[1] After Major Freeland, there was Elijah P. Lovejoy, publisher, who, because of a mishap regarding some type, whipped William so severely he needed five weeks to recover. Next was Otis Reynolds, a steamboat captain who hired William to wait on gentlemen. Though Reynolds was a kind employer and the job was pleasant, William began to think seriously of escape because, as he says, "in passing from place to place, and seeing new faces every day, and knowing that they could go where they pleased, I soon became unhappy, and several times thought of leaving the boat at some landing place, and trying to make my escape to Canada, which I had heard much about as a place where the slave might be free, and be protected." He would not, however, leave his mother. Eventually, Reynolds left the boat and William returned to Mr. Young, who sent him to work in his corn fields. Soon, however, William was hired out again, this time to Mr. Walker, a "soul-driver" who transported slaves to New Orleans for auction. It was William's job to see that slaves ready for sale appeared cheerful and happy, to "set them to dancing when their cheeks were wet with tears." Once, having provoked Walker, he was told to deliver a message to the jail. Suspicious, he asked a passerby to read him the note, and, when he learned he was to be whipped, paid another slave to deliver it: "this incident shows how it is that slavery makes its victims lying and mean; for which vices it afterwards reproaches them, and uses them as arguments to prove that they deserve no better fate." When his contract with Walker expired, William returned to Mr. Young, who, having determined to sell William to get some much needed money, gave him one week to find a new master who would buy him. Since his sister had already been sold away and his mother finally consented to join him, William took this opportunity to escape north and find a new "master" in Canada. But they were captured in Illinois and returned to St. Louis. Brown's mother was sold further south and he never saw her again. Brown himself was sold to a Mr. Willi, who in turn sold him to a Captain Price.

It was while he was traveling with Mr. and Mrs. Price along the Ohio River that Brown made his second attempt at escape. He traveled by night, rested by day. Eventually starvation and cold *threatened his life, forcing him to seek aid from a man dressed as a Quaker. The Wells Browns welcomed him, fed and clothed him, and then sent him on his way to Cleveland where he found work on the boats conveying fugitive slaves across Lake Erie to Canada. Eventually, he joined the abolitionist movement.*

Thirteen years later, the ex-slave, now called William Wells Brown, wrote his Narrative, *dedicating it to Wells Brown. Mr. J.C. Hathaway, president of the Western New York Anti-slavery Society, introduced the narrative:*

> *The friends of freedom may well congratulate each other on the appearance of the following Narrative. It adds another volume to the rapidly increasing anti-slavery literature of the age. It has been remarked by a close observer of human nature, "Let me make the songs of a nation, and I care not who makes its laws;" and it may with equal truth be said, that, among a reading people like our own, their books will at least give character to their laws. It is an influence which goes forth noiselessly upon its mission, but fails not to find its way to many a warm heart, to kindle on the altar thereof the fires of freedom, which will one day break forth in a living flame to consume oppression.*
>
> *This little book is a voice from the prison-house, unfolding the deeds of darkness which are there perpetrated. Our cause has received efficient aid from this source. The names of those who have come from thence, and battled manfully for the right, need not to be recorded here. The works of some of them are an enduring monument of praise, and their perpetual record shall be found in the grateful hearts of the redeemed bondman.* (vii)

I

Slave narratives were an extremely popular form of literature in the nineteenth century, especially after 1831 when the antislavery crusade began operating full force. Thousands of narratives came into print, some to be published in abolitionist periodicals, others separately bound. According to Charles H. Nichols, Jr.,

> they were so popular that almost any victim of slavery could get published. Among these were manumitted slaves like Sojourner Truth, those who had bought themselves, like Moses Grandy, and many fugitives, like Frederick Douglass. A large number of narratives were issued as paper bound pamphlets and sold for twenty-five cents. The longer and better bound ones could be had for a dollar and a half. *The Interesting Narrative of the Life of Olaudah Equiano or Gusteves Vassa, The African* went into at least ten editions by 1837; a Dutch and a German edition are extant. At least six editions of Charles Ball's *Slavery in the United States* were issued between 1836 and 1859. By 1856 the *Narrative of Moses Roper's Adventures and Escape from American Slavery,* first published in 1837, had reached ten editions and had been translated into Celtic. Josiah Henson's narrative had sold six thousand copies in 1852, by having been published in England as well as in America. By 1858 advanced orders for the "Stowe edition" of Henson's book totalled 5,000 copies. In the 1878 edition it is claimed that 100,000 copies of the earlier book had been sold. Henson's life story was translated into Dutch and into French. Within two years after its publications in 1853 *The Narrative of Solomon Northup* had sold 27,000 copies. *The Narrative of William Wells Brown* sold 8,000 copies by 1849, and Douglass' narrative had, by the same year, gone through seven editions. So widespread was the circula-

tion of these autobiographies that Olmsted remarked that Northern views of the peculiar institution were largely derived from the narratives of the fugitive slaves.[2]

Their popularity must have been due in part to their appeal as tales of thrilling adventures. But more than that, they offered northern readers, many of them descendants of Puritans and Quakers, a very literal description of the flight of the soul from bondage in the hell of slavery. As Arna Bontemps suggests: "The recorded memoirs of the questing slave were felt by many readers of the nineteenth century to epitomize the condition of man on the earth as it documented the personal history of the individual to whom bondage was real and freedom was more than a dream."[3]

Because of their appeal to the reader on such religious and moral grounds, the slave narratives were powerful political weapons for converting people to the abolitionist cause. Frederick Douglass justified his own autobiography, which he feared would bring charges against him of pretentiousness, on the basis of its political usefulness. In a letter to his editor he wrote:

It is not to illustrate any heroic achievements of a man, but to vindicate a just and beneficent principle, in its application to the whole human family, by letting in the light of truth upon a system, esteemed by some as a blessing, and by others as a curse and a crime. I agree with you, that this system is now at the bar of public opinion—not only of this country, but of the whole civilized world—for judgment. Its friends have made for it the usual plea—"not guilty;" the case must, therefore, proceed. Any facts, either from slaves, slaveholders, or by-standers calculated to enlighten the public mind, by revealing the true nature, character, and tendency of the slave system, are in order, and can scarcely be innocently withheld.[4]

Douglass, Brown, and other slave narrators very deliberately accumulated diverse materials—anecdotes of friends and relatives, newspaper clippings, work descriptions, character sketches, sections of the slave code—in order to illuminate vividly all aspects and ramifications of the total socio-political-economic-psychological environment. In Brown's *Narrative*, for example, each incident takes the form of a digression that interrupts the main line of narration (his own life and escape). The accumulative impact of the digressive material renders the grim reality of slavery inescapable. In this way, the slave narrative functioned as an early form of protest literature, whose purpose was to expose the nature of the slave system and to provide moral instruction through the vehicle of autobiography, perhaps the most effective one since it personalized the argument, rendering the experience immediate and concrete rather than abstract and general.

The use of these narratives for abolitionist politics (and for economic gain) had certain inescapable ramifications.[5] First of all, it affected their quality. Many of the narratives were hastily thrown together, loosely structured, episodic accounts lacking any controlling point of view.[6] This was not universally the case, however. The narrative of William and Ellen Craft is a spellbinding account of what must be one of the most bizarre escape journeys in all of slave literature. Certainly the narratives of Brown, Douglass, and Henry Bibb are imaginatively drawn and perceptively controlled, revealing as they do a sophisticated integration of precise detail and insightful generalization. Second, such political motivations affect the veracity of the slave narratives. Many of them were dictated by ex-slaves to white ghost writers, abolitionists who may have had good intentions but nevertheless took license to render the narrative as effective a propaganda tract as possible. In fact, some narratives were total fabrications, a discovery that served slavery's advocates well since they could then argue that the narratives lied about the nature of the slave system. (After the fraudulent narratives had been exposed, however, most abolitionists were careful to corroborate the stories they printed.) Be that as it may, the slave narrator during the period before the Civil War had more latitude in the choice of narrative thrust and detail than his successor, who would be bound to the whims of less sympathetic publishers and readers.

At the same time that the narratives protested the slave system, they offered a countercharge to slavery advocates' claims of Negro inferiority by testifying to the sophistication and educability of the race. Douglass continues in his letter to his editor:

I see, too, that there are special reasons why I should write my own biography, in preference to employing another to do it. Not only is slavery on trial, but unfortunately, the enslaved people are also on trial. It is alleged, that they are, naturally, inferior; that they are *so low* in the scale of humanity, and so utterly stupid, that they are unconscious of their wrongs, and do not apprehend their rights. Looking, then, at your request, from this standpoint, and wishing everything of which you think me capable to go to the benefit of my afflicted people, I part with my doubts and hesitation, and proceed to furnish you the desired manuscript. . . . (vii)

The act of writing an autobiography was yet another act of rebellion against the slave system, for the choice of autobiography presupposes a belief in the primacy of the self. In writing autobiography, the ex-slave affirmed his belief in his self-worth and forced a society that had denied him full humanity to recognize him. These public-political impulses have continued to be motivating forces behind black autobiography.

The writing of the narratives fulfilled certain private needs for the ex-slave also. By reenacting his life story, he could reaffirm the significance of his struggle to free himself. Then, too, in the very process of narrating his particular experience, the sophisticated ex-slave developed an analysis of the larger system out of which his individual experience evolved. That Brown and Douglass, for instance, were as concerned about making statements about the system as they were about relating the events of their lives has already been noted as one of the primary public impulses. But the implications involved here are private as well, for in the process of generalizing from his particular history, the narrator was shaping his analysis of the institution of American slavery. To the extent that he developed an analysis, he came to a greater understanding of himself as a product of the forces he had analyzed. This impulse to use autobiography as a means to develop an analysis of America's racism, through which the black American comes to understand himself more fully, has continued into the present, as we will see in later chapters.

The slave narrative represented in itself a spiritual transcendence over the brutalizing experience of slavery. In the act of writing, the slave narrator could again liberate himself from slavery—in this case the spiritual slavery of the past rather than the physical slavery of the South. He achieved this spiritual liberation by giving distance to the pain of the past through the imposition of artistic form on the matter of experience, thus gaining control and mastery over it. Two brief passages from Brown's narrative suggest the extent of his own control of the past through various techniques. The first is a self-portrait:

> My master had family worship, night and morning. At night, the slaves were called in to attend; but in the mornings, they had to be at their work, and master did all the praying. My master and mistress were great lovers of mint julep, and every morning, a pitcher-full was made, of which they all partook freely, not excepting little master William. After drinking freely all around, they would have family worship, and then breakfast. I cannot say but I loved the julep as well as any of them, and during prayer was always careful to seat myself close to the table where it stood, so as to help myself when they were all busily engaged in their devotions. By the time prayer was over, I was about as happy as any of them. (37)

In recreating his past, Brown must, of course, recreate himself as the protagonist of his life story. Through his approach to the material of this self-portrait—the objective description of the circumstances, the refusal to editorialize or moralize, the honesty, and the humor—he maintains a controlled distance between himself in the present as writer and himself in the past as protagonist, a distance that allows him to recognize and portray the full absurdity of his situation and therefore to affirm his full humanity. The objectivity achieved and the selfhood affirmed are the final and, in many ways, the most enduring testament of freedom.

While the above passage puts his own previous role in a certain perspective, the following passage gives distance even to the most brutal acts of the slaveholder. Brown describes a meeting with a notoriously cruel slaveholder:

> As we were driving past the house of D. D. Page, a gentleman who owned a large baking establishment, as I was sitting upon the box of the carriage, which was very much elevated, I saw Mr. Page pursuing a slave around the yard, with a long whip, cutting him at every jump. The man soon escaped from the yard, and was followed by Mr. Page. They came running past us, and the slave perceiving that he would be overtaken, stopped suddenly, and Page stumbled over him, and falling on the stone pavement, fractured one of his legs, which crippled him for life. The same gentleman, but a short time previous, tied up a woman of his, by the name of Delphia, and whipped her nearly to death. (38-39)

The objectivity of the description and the refusal to moralize render the reality all the more devastating. But Brown is not yet finished, for he comments further:

> Yet he was a deacon in the Baptist Church, in good and regular standing. Poor Delphia! I was well acquainted with her, and called to see her while upon her sick bed; and I shall never forget her appearance. She was a member of the same church with her master. (39)

The irony, of course, emanates from the recognition of the incongruity between the actual cruelty and the ideal of Christian brotherhood and is effectively underscored by the brevity of the comment. In his rigid control of emotion through irony, the narrator masters and gives artistic form to the turbulence of emotion lurking beneath the surface.

This careful control through distancing, this rite of order-ing, could be personally redemptive for those who escaped from a system as destructive of the personality as slavery. In other words, artistic distancing becomes a means of survival through which the narrator transcends the absurd incon-gruities of reality at the same time as those incongruities are fully confronted. This possibility of liberation through literary expression continues into the present and becomes especially meaningful as other kinds of escape prove un-successful.

II

Brown, as did Frederick Douglass and Henry Bibb, the Crafts, and every other slave narrator, offered the reader his personal variation on the general theme. To survive in the South where he was labeled a chattel and thereby stripped of his humanity, condemned to inferiority, and denied uniqueness, the slave had to suppress all needs of legitimate self-assertion, all aspirations of self-fulfillment; in other words, the self had to be sacrificed or "lost" in order for it to be "saved"—physically. In response to such oppres-sion, Brown and all other escaped slaves chose by their own willed act of self-affirmation to flee. The controlling motif in the slave narrative, therefore, is the "freeing" of an authentic identity from the chains of the false one foisted upon the slave by southern society.

Accordingly, the structural pattern imposed by the nar-rator upon his past describes a journey toward freedom: a *break away from* the enslavement of one society and the *break into* the "better day" of another. This journey is simultan-eously a physical or geographical one—to the North—and a spiritual one—to acceptance into society as a human being and thus to the possibility of legitimate selfhood. The slave narrative embodies two directional movements: alienation and flight from one society and (theoretically or hopefully) integration and acceptance into another. Within this general framework interweave several recurrent motifs, representative of the experience of Brown and the other escaped slaves and prototypal of the motifs of later black autobiography, although, as will become evident, with each new generation and each new autobiographer, the emphases will shift, the complexities proliferate.

Masking: A Rite of Endurance

For the slave, self-assertion was self-defeating. It more than likely meant mutilation; it often meant death. As a youth, Brown witnessed the fate of Randall, a powerful slave who had escaped the lash because he was valuable and because he was determined no white man would whip him. Cook, the overseer, was just as determined to subdue him. Unsuccessful alone, Cook enlisted the aid of three men.

> They came up to where Randall was at work, and Cook ordered him to leave his work, and go with them to the barn. He refused to go; whereupon he was attacked by the overseer and his companions, when he turned upon them, and laid them, one after another, prostrate on the ground. Woodbridge drew out his pistol and fired at him, and brought him to the ground by a pistol ball. The others rushed upon him with their clubs, and beat him over the head and face, until they succeeded in tying him. He was then taken to the barn, and tied to a beam. Cook gave him over one hundred lashes with a heavy cowhide, had him washed with salt and water, and left him tied during the day. The next day he was

untied, and taken to a blacksmith's shop, and had a ball and chain attached to his leg. He was compelled to labor in the field, and perform the same amount of work that the other hands did. When his master returned home, he was much pleased to find that Randall had been subdued in his absence. (20)

Yet not all the offenses of self-assertion for which the slave received punishment were, like Randall's, manifestations of sheer physical power. Early in his autobiography, Frederick Douglass delineates more subtle nuances of this crime. A woman named Nelly is whipped for "one of the commonest and most indefinite . . . offenses, . . . 'impudence' ":

This may mean almost anything, or nothing at all, just according to the caprice of the master or overseer, at the moment. But, whatever it is, or is not, if it gets the name of "impudence," the party charged with it is sure of a flogging. This offense may be committed in various ways; in the tone of an answer; in answering at all; in not answering; in the expression of countenance; in the motion of the head; in the gait, manner, and bearing of the slave. (92)

The alternative to self-assertion was the fabrication of a mask, prerequisite for a less onerous existence, even for sheer survival itself. The slave learned to perfect the game of "puttin' on ole Massa!". Deceit, cunning, fawning ingratiation, stupidity—these were only some of the many faces of his mask, a subtle psychological device to prevent the master from knowing what was really happening in the mind and heart of the "darky."

The ramifications of masking were potentially enslaving

and liberating. On the one hand, the individual, unable to express himself authentically, could do so only obliquely through the acrobatics of his mask. In sacrificing himself to this mask, the slave therefore risked becoming alienated from and irresponsive to his real self. He was thus doubly enslaved, politically in the South and psychologically within his mask. But masking also assumed certain positive ramifications: first, and most fundamental, the mask was a means of survival; second, and psychologically no less important, the mask was an oblique means of rebellion within the system as the black slave became a confidence man par excellence. From the knowledge that he was outwitting "ole massa" the slave could derive a limited but very real sense of power over his circumstance. And in an existence otherwise characterized by absolute impotence, this mode of expression, this mastery over the master, became a form of self-dignity, an alternative form of freedom within enslavement.

For the slave plotting escape, this oblique form of freedom ensured the possibility of the achievement of real freedom. "Ever after I entertained the first idea of being free," writes Lunsford Lane,

> I had endeavored so to conduct myself as not to become obnoxious to the white inhabitants, knowing as I did their power, and their hostility to the colored people. The two points necessary in such a case I had kept constantly in mind. First, I had made no display of the little property or money I possessed, but in every way I wore as much as possible the aspect of poverty. Second, I had never appeared to be even so intelligent as I really was. This all colored people at the south, free and slaves, find it peculiarly necessary to their own comfort and safety to observe.[7]

Flight: A Rite of Passage

No matter how desperate the reality of southern slavery, the slave hoped for the "better day." For those slaves resigned to their fate, this better day would come only after death. But for those rebellious ones who refused to submit abjectly to slavery, that better day was the very real day they abandoned the South for the freedom of the North. For William Wells Brown, it was January 1, 1834. There could be hope precisely because there was a "place" to escape to. Central to the slave narrative is a firm sense of direction—of a place left and a goal to be attained. Brown writes that after his escape from the river boat he

> walked up and down the road until near midnight, when the clouds disappeared, and I welcomed the sight of my friend,—truly the slave's friend—the North Star.
> As soon as I saw it, I knew my course, and before daylight I travelled twenty or twenty-five miles. (96)

Once escaped he had to resolve the difficulties along his way—cold, hunger, inadequate clothing, fear of kidnappers; but they were endurable, even surmountable, obstacles because the slave knew that freedom lay ahead. The fear of capture and return only made him more firm in his resolve. Unfortunately for later black autobiographers, this firm sense of freedom becomes elusive—if not completely illusive.

The geographical line between Kentucky and Ohio, between Maryland and New York or Pennsylvania, was the point of the radical break from an enslaved to a free identity, a break that was political as well as personal. The act of running was in fact a criminal act: the slave who attempted to escape or succeeded was going outside the laws of society since escaping was an extreme form of theft, the most dramatic violation of property rights. For the slave and the slave narrator, this criminal activity, like masking, had a positive value: by running, he rescued himself from spiritual and psychological death.

And so the running slave took on some of the attributes of the romantic rebel, although it would be misleading to construe this flight as metaphysical. He fled southern society in order to transcend a false identity; thus, he was forced to rebel, forced to play outlaw. Yet the slave was committed, when committed to anything but survival and necessity, to democratic social values. Believing in his equality and individuality, he fled toward another society where he believed he could express himself freely. Prolonged physical, social, and psychological alienation from one society led him to seek acceptance and integration into northern society as confirmation of his selfhood. His flight was, thus, political rather than metaphysical, for it was not the wilderness but the community that could grant the ex-slave political freedom: the outsider fled in order to become an insider.

Naming: A Rite of Rebirth

The slavocracy, in order to insure successful subordination of the black slaves, exercised the conqueror's power to proscribe learning in general and names in particular. The slaves were stripped of their past, its language and traditions, and forced to learn only what the slaveholders thought safe for them to learn. As Gilbert Osofsky notes in his introduction to a collection of slave narratives, "the 'word' has quasi-magical, mystical connotations. The right to control it is the power to order reality, to subjugate man himself."[8] The slaves were named according to the status they bore in American society. If they were given Christian names—a practice significant in itself because it emphasized the Westernization of the slaves and the justification often put forth in defense of slavery (that the Christianizing of the savages was the white man's burden)—these names were first names only. The slave invariably lacked the last name, the one we associate with family history and thus with respectability; or, if he did have two names, one would be the master's name either first in possessive form, as, for example, Johnson's Tom, or vice versa, Tom Johnson. Such naming symbolized his relationship to a society that reduced some human beings to mere possessions.

Not only was the act of naming a possessive one; it was also a capricious one as this illustration from Solomon Northup's *Narrative* testifies. Theophilus Freeman, a slaver in charge of transporting Northup and other slaves belonging to a man named Burch, demands of the captain, "Where's Platt?"

> The captain was unable to inform him, no one being on board answering to that name.
>
> "Who shipped *that* nigger?" he again inquired of the captain, pointing to me.
>
> "Burch," replied the captain.
>
> "Your name is Platt—you answer my description. Why don't you come forward?" he demanded of me, in an angry tone.
>
> I informed him that was not my name; that I had never been called by it, but that I had no objection to it as I knew of.
>
> "Well, I will learn you your name," said he; "and so you won't forget it either, by—," he added.[9]

In this way, the slave's sense of identity had to be readjusted continually because such identity was fluid, always subject to the whims of society. In this way, the slavocracy maintained its power to subordinate him because it had the power to determine who he was. As an orphan as well as a bastard, he had no stable family context from which to derive support, no father from whom to inherit his identity. Brown could only write: "My father's name, as I learned from my mother, was George Higgins. He was a white man, a relative of my master, and connected with some of the first families in Kentucky" (13).

Rebelling against such systematic deindividualization, reveling in his new freedom, the ex-slave named himself anew. Brown is thus understandably anxious to assume a new name. Originally, his name had been William, but the nephew of his master was a "William" and so Brown's mother had been ordered to change her son's name to "Sanford," one to which he never adapted. Thus, immediately after the tension of the actual escape passed, "Sanford" concerns himself with this very process of naming:

> As soon as the subject came to my mind, I resolved on adopting my old name of William, and let Sanford go by the board, for I always hated it. Not because there was anything peculiar in the name; but because it had been forced upon me. It is sometimes common at the south, for slaves to take the name of their masters. Some have a legitimate right to do so. But I always detested the idea of being called by the name of either of my masters. And as for my father, I would rather have adopted the name of "Friday," and been known as the servant of some Robinson Crusoe, than to have taken his name. So I was not only hunting for my

liberty, but also hunting for a name; though I regarded the latter as of little consequence, if I could but gain the former. Travelling along the road, I would sometimes speak to myself, sounding my name over, by way of getting used to it, before I should arrive among civilized human beings. (98-99)

In repossessing his former name and rejecting an identity foisted upon him by society, he asserts his new-found freedom. The rite of naming was thus a central experience that came to symbolize the act of liberation. His new identity, however, to be valid, must be complemented with a last name: this final rite of passage is performed by the Quaker Wells Brown:

Before leaving this good Quaker friend, he inquired what my name was besides William. I told him that I had no other name. "Well," said he, "thee must have another name. Since thee has got out of slavery, thee has become a man, and men always have two names."

I told him that he was the first man to extend the hand of friendship to me, and I would give him the privilege of naming me.

"If I name thee," said he, "I shall call thee Wells Brown, after myself."

"But," said I, "I am not willing to lose my name of William. As it was taken from me once against my will, I am not willing to part with it again upon any terms."

"Then," said he, "I will call thee William Wells Brown."

"So be it," said I. (106)

Thus Brown is offered a last name (respectability) by a

representative of a society that accepts him "as a man." The baptismal rite of naming symbolizes his baptism into a "free" life, his achievement of "place."

Mastery: A Rite of Entry

In escaping North, both the male and female slave fled from physical exploitation to physical self-mastery, for the system functioned to psychically emasculate the male slave who dared not under threat of punishment, perhaps even death, assert his masculinity against the master or overseer, and to exploit the female slave who had to surrender her body on demand. Impotent when attacked, powerless when violated, both male and female slave had no recourse but to succumb and acquiesce, losing the respect of those around them, ultimately losing their own self-respect.

Occasionally the slave was driven to self-defense. While working for the ruthless overseer Covey, Douglass is whipped for fainting and, in response, runs away for several days. When he returns on the Sabbath, Covey does nothing. Monday morning, however, he attacks, at which time Douglass recalls his "pledge *to stand up in my own defense*" and fights back—successfully:

> Well, my dear reader, this battle with Mr. Covey, —undignified as it was, and as I fear my narration of it is—was the turning point in my *"life as a slave."* It rekindled in my breast the smouldering embers of liberty; it brought up my Baltimore dreams, and revived a sense of my own manhood. I was a changed being after that fight. I was *nothing* before; I WAS A MAN NOW. It recalled to life my crushed self-respect and my self-confidence, and inspired me with a renewed determination to be A FREEMAN. A man,

without force, is without the essential dignity of humanity. Human nature is so constituted, that it cannot *honor* a helpless man, although it can *pity* him; and even this it cannot do long, if the signs of power do not arise. (247)

Douglass calls this moment "the turning point" of his life, recognizing it as the moment when the individual chooses to rebel against the social status quo and recover his manhood, no matter what the cost. Rarely was the cost as minimal as it was in Douglass' case.

Nonetheless, until he fled North, the slave was condemned to spiritual childhood, a reality Douglass recognized only too clearly: "The thought of only being a creature of the *present* and the *past*," he writes, "troubled me, and I longed to have a *future*—a future with hope in it. To be shut up entirely in the past and present, is abhorrent to the human mind; it is to the soul—whose life and happiness is unceasing progress—what the prison is to the body" (273). Of course, the most insidious consequence of the myth of inferiority, which functioned to justify slavery, involved the psychic collaboration of the slave himself: to be treated as inferior and to be constantly reminded of that inferiority—through punishment, forced labor, religious argument—could lead, not surprisingly, to an acquiescence to it. Fortunately, the escaped slave never acquiesced. And so, no matter how good the master, the rebellious slave sought to become his own. Douglass admits: "To the credit of Mr. Freeland . . . it must be stated, that he was the best master I ever had, until I became my own master, and assumed for myself as I had a right to do, the responsibility of my own existence and the exercise of my own powers" (268).

No longer condemned to perpetual insignificance as a

slave, the black American could realize and fulfill himself through a meaningful social role: private visions could become public realities. A freeman, he could participate in the secular drama of selfhood by rising from his beginnings to a place of value and prominence within society, reenacting in his own way, the American dream of self-improvement. Douglass is perhaps the best known of the slave narrators who achieved prominence in American society, first as abolitionist and later as foreign ambassador.

However, as a member of the black community as well as the greater American community, the escaped slave often chose a social vocation devoted to improving the situation of the black American. His exhilaration in his new status must have been tempered by his knowledge that those he left behind, strangers as well as relatives, were not as fortunate as he. Having himself successfully broken into northern society, the escapee redirected his energies into the cause of abolition, publicly by speaking and pamphleteering, privately by returning South to lead others to freedom or by earning the money to buy family and friends from slavery.

Expatriation: The Elusiveness of Freedom

The slave narrative is apparently a narrative of success. But there is also another story implicit, if not actually explicit, within the slave narrative. That story is the story of failure to find real freedom and acceptance within American society, a disturbing sequel to the successful story of the radical break away from southern society. From the point of view of later black autobiography, there is a final ironic dimension in William Wells Brown's baptismal rite of naming—a complexity of which Brown could not possibly have been aware but of which later autobiographers will be only too well aware. Wells Brown names William after him-self, and Brown symbolically represents free northern soci-ety. How much different is this act of naming from the southern practice of giving the slave the master's name —Tom Johnson or Johnson's Tom? Wells Brown, in a very revealing sense, is possessing the ex-slave, as did his south-ern counterpart, by determining his identity. Ironically even northern society imprisons the ex-slave through its possessiveness. This is the cruelest irony of all: the freed slave is not free in the North. Freedom is merely a chimera.

Granted, the northern black was free of master and over-seer, of auction block and arbitrary separation from family. He could even improve his social position in the North. But Solomon Northup's experience clearly dramatizes the il-lusory nature of the free sanctuary of the North. Born a free slave in New York, he was kidnapped by slavers and sold down South: thirteen years later he finally regained his freedom. Other ex-slaves lived with this lurking threat of recapture. Then in 1850, Congress passed the Fugitive Slave Bill, requiring northerners not only to refuse assis-tance to escaped slaves but to assist in returning them to the South.

Leon F. Litwack in his study *North of Slavery* discusses extensively the real limitations of black American freedom in the North—political, economic, educational, and religious—and concludes that white supremacy reigned in the North as it did in the South. The community of abolitionists that accepted the slave as an equal was a very small community indeed, and even it argued the feasibility of Negro membership in the movement. Such debates re-flected the acknowledgment of differences between the races, so that it was often the abolitionists themselves who perpetuated the projective stereotypes of the Negro.[10] Moreover, practical considerations often clashed with the individual ex-slave's needs for self-improvement, a dilemma Douglass dramatizes when he discusses his speaking efforts:

> It was impossible for me to repeat the same old story month after month, and to keep my interest in it. . . . "Tell your story, Frederick," would whisper my then revered friend, William Lloyd Garrison, as I stepped upon the platform. I could not always obey, for I was now reading and thinking. New views of the subject were presented to my mind. It did not entirely satisfy me to *narrate* wrongs; I felt like *denouncing* them. I could not always curb my moral indignation for the perpetrators of slave-holding villainy, long enough for a circumstantial statement of the facts which I felt almost everyone must know. Besides I was growing, and needed room. "People won't believe you ever was a slave, Frederick, if you keep on this way," said Friend Foster. (361-362)

Even in the North, even in the abolitionist community, the black American met opposition to his quest after self-realization.

And so the ex-slave moved on again. Expatriation became the answer for some. After finding that agents were in Boston to return him South, William Wells Brown fled to England. So did William and Ellen Craft. From England, the Crafts concluded their account with the following indictment: "In short, it is well known in England, if not all over the world, that the Americans, as a people, are notoriously mean and cruel towards all colored persons, whether they are bond or free."[11]

Notes

[1] William Wells Brown, *Narrative of the Life of William W. Brown, A Fugitive Slave: Written by Himself,* pp. 21-22. Further citations will appear in the text.

[2] Charles H. Nichols, Jr., *Many Thousand Gone,* pp. xiv-xv.

[3] Arna Bontemps, ed., *Great Slave Narratives,* p. vii.

[4] Frederick Douglass, *My Bondage and My Freedom,* p. vii. Further citations will appear in the text.

[5] The ex-slave often needed to make money quickly so that he could buy family and friends from slavery.

[6] See Margaret Young Jackson, "An Investigation of Biographies and Autobiographies of American Slaves Published between 1840 and 1860," chap. VI.

[7] Lunsford Lane, *The Narrative of Lunsford Lane,* p. 31.

[8] Gilbert Osofsky, ed., *Puttin' on Ole Massa,* p. 41.

[9] Solomon Northup, *Twelve Years a Slave,* p. 61.

[10] Leon F. Litwack, *North of Slavery,* p. 224.

[11] William Craft, *Running a Thousand Miles for Freedom,* p. 87.

2

CASTING DOWN

Here upon this stage the black rite of Horatio Alger was performed to God's own acting script.
            —Ralph Ellison, Invisible Man

During slavery, the journey toward freedom was a geographical one: change of place was enough. Then when the Civil War brought an end to slavery, "everyplace" in America was to become a symbolic North. Theoretically a free American, the black was about to benefit from all the privileges of that identity; former dreams were to become realities. A change of place would no longer be necessary. For a while, the exhilaration of Reconstruction prolonged the exuberance of the new order; but, ominously, the promise of that new order gave way before the repressive measures of the late nineteenth century. Patterns of disenfranchisement, segregation, and racial subordination became the new way of life: the slave system was merely replaced with the race system. Thus, as the experience of the escaped slave prophesied, freedom was a chimera. The black American, though he was no longer three-fifths of a human being, was only three-fifths of a citizen. Consequently, he found himself plagued by a dual identity and dual reality—the promised reality of full American citizenship and the daily reality of the status of a Negro that belied that promise. The socially determined identity that had plagued him as a slave, imprisoning him in the stereotypes of white America, prevailed, condemning him to invisibility: "One was never told, 'You are a man.' It was always, 'You are a Negro,'" remembers J. Saunders Redding.[1] *Still a bastard in his own country, the black continued his quest for freedom; only now it became much more complex, much more ambiguous.*

Thus the autobiography of the black American has continued to be a form of slave narrative. The two patterns inherent in the slave narrative, however, tend to separate. On the one hand, there is the story of a successful break into *the community, a reenactment of America's secular drama of selfhood. This autobiographical tradition reflects, through the story of a social calling, the slave narrative's focus on the achievement of place within northern society. On the other hand, there is the story of the* break away *from the imprisoning community, a reenactment of the sacred quest for selfhood. Hence, this tradition reflects more the initial direction of the slave narrative and the later illusory nature of the achievement of freedom.*

In the secular pattern, the autobiographer reviews the events of his life from the vantage point of achieved success, imposing upon them a pattern of movement toward fame: having legitimized himself by becoming a respected member of society—as entertainer, athlete, artist, social leader, political figure—he has achieved a viable form of freedom. Precisely because the autobiographer considers this fulfillment a result of his social calling, he focuses on the achievements of his public self, gleaning the chaotic past experience of his life for those significant moments relevant to his choice of and success in that calling, shaping them into a work whose purpose is to make a statement about how his life led to such an achievement of "place" within society. He may choose several points at which to end: the moment at which he chose his calling or, more likely, the moment of a major success that was particularly meaningful to him as a culmination of his earlier efforts.

Often underlying this structural pattern in American autobiography is the myth of the Horatio Alger hero, a manifestation of the secularization of puritanism first embodied in Benjamin Franklin's Autobiography. *From a lowly beginning on the fringes of society, the hard-working and virtuous individual rises slowly yet steadily to success and social prominence: self-realization is fulfilled by social arrival. In this traditional myth of American identity, the individual's relationship to society is fluid, and his possibilities are unlimited. For the black American, this pattern becomes especially expressive and often painfully ironic since he begins on the furthest fringe of the social scale (the fluidity of his movement is problematic) and the odds against him are greater (his unlimited possibilities are in fact narrowly limited). In reenacting the successful struggle with his background and his society, he reinforces and reaffirms the "American" side of his dual identity. Freedom becomes synonymous with the ability to participate in the American myth of democratic possibility.*

I

Booker T. Washington was probably the first well-known black Horatio Alger. "By the beginning of the new century, Washington," explains John Hope Franklin in an introduction to one edition of the autobiography,

. . . was one of the most powerful men in the United States. Great philanthropists and industrialists such as

Andrew Carnegie and John D. Rockefeller listened to him courteously and were influenced by his advice. Presidents such as Theodore Roosevelt and William Howard Taft depended on him for suggestions regarding the resolution of problems involving race. Southern whites in high places knew that a good word in their behalf by Washington would open doors previously closed to them.[2]

After achieving such stature and power in American society, Washington was urged by others to write his autobiography. The popularity of *Up From Slavery,* which became a best seller soon after publication, indicated how inspiring his rise to fame had been.[3] His life was an embodiment of the possibility of self-improvement, made powerful and tangible by his preference for objective reality. "I have great faith in the power and influence of facts," writes Washington early in the work.[4]

I have found, too, that it is the visible, the tangible, that goes a long ways in softening prejudice. The actual sight of a first-class house that a Negro has built is ten times more potent than pages of discussion about a house that he ought to build, or perhaps could build. (154)

His exemplary life is just such a tangible "house," and the narrative of his rise to fame is designed to relate the material facts of its evolutionary construction within society.

A sense of mystery pervades the first paragraph of the autobiography. Washington does not know the exact place or date of his birth; he "suspects [he] must have been born somewhere and at some time" (1). To this initial sense of

mystery, the second paragraph adds the quality of life
—desolate poverty—and the third paragraph his anony-
mous ancestry. Although Washington knew his mother's
name, he admits: "Of my father I knew even less than of my
mother. I do not even know his name" (2). The prominent
leader enters the drama of life as a semi-orphan, spawned
mysteriously from nowhere, secured by no ancestral roots,
environed by humble conditions. This beginning sharpens
the contrast with his social position fifty years later at the
time of writing and underscores the fact that whatever he
achieved he achieved single-handedly.

Soon after emancipation, Washington, as did other
former slaves, named himself. The child's choice of name is
particularly revealing: by naming himself "Washington"
—a name associated with patriotism, American democracy,
social prominence, and leadership—Booker, prompted by
a belief in the society into which he was born and a need to
be a part of and a leader in that society, creates an ideal
identity which embodies his personal vision of himself.
Naming becomes a prophetic, baptismal ritual.

The next rite of passage of Washington's journey is the
"effort to fit [himself] to accomplish the most good in the
world" (51). The early part of his narrative, therefore,
centers on his struggle to secure an education, first at
Kanawha Valley school and then at Hampton Institute,
which, interestingly enough, he describes as "the promised
land." Thereafter, the autobiography becomes the narrative of Washington's work, an open-ended exposition of his
public efforts to better the conditions of his race, especially
through the founding and growth of Tuskegee Institute.
He focuses his narrative, as he did his life, on the material
obstacles he had to overcome—money to finance new build-
ings, furniture, clothing for the students, and so on and on.
In the process of surmounting these obstacles, Washington

assumes the position of leadership which fulfills the destiny inherent in the name.

The many parallels between Washington's success story and that of Benjamin Franklin are striking and suggest the degree to which Washington is simply giving us the black version of a well-known formula. Both men, growing restless at an early age because their overwhelming need for self-improvement remains unsatisfied, journey to a distant city that offers them an opportunity to fulfill that need. Both describe their entry into the city similarly, stressing, by implication, the disparity between their early status and their prominence at the moment of writing. Here is Franklin's entrance into Philadelphia in 1723:

> I have been the more particular in this description of my journey, and shall be so of my first entry into that city, that you may in your mind compare such unlikely beginnings with the figure I have since made there. I was in my working dress, my best clothes being to come round by sea. I was dirty from my journey; my pockets were stuffed out with shirts and stockings; I knew no soul, nor where to look for lodging. Fatigued with walking, rowing, and want of rest, I was very hungry, and my whole stock of cash consisted of a Dutch dollar and about a shilling in copper coin, which I gave to the boatmen for my passage. At first they refused it on account of my having rowed; but I insisted on their taking it. A man is sometimes more generous when he has little money than when he has plenty, perhaps through fear of being thought to have but little. I walked towards the top of the street, gazing about till near Market Street, where I met a boy with bread. I have often made a meal of dry bread, and inquiring where he had bought it, I went immediately to the

baker's he directed me to. I asked for bisket, meaning such as we had in Boston; but that sort, it seems, was not made in Philadelphia. I then asked for a three penny loaf and was told they had none such. Not knowing the different prices nor the names of the different sorts of bread, I told him to give me three pennyworth of any sort. He gave me accordingly three great puffy rolls. I was surprised at the quantity but took it, and having no room in my pockets, walked off with a roll under each arm and eating the other. Thus I went up Market Street as far as Fourth Street, passing by the door of Mr. Read, my future wife's father; when she, standing at the door, saw me, and thought I made—as I certainly did—a most awkward, ridiculous appearance. Then I turned and went down Chestnut Street and part of Walnut Street, eating my roll all the way, and coming round, found myself again at Market Street wharf near the boat I came in, to which I went for a draught of the river water, and being filled with one of my rolls, gave the other two to a woman and her child that came down the river in the boat with us and were waiting to go farther.[5]

Washington's description of his entry into Richmond in 1872 echoes Franklin's self-portraiture and his chronology of concerns:

By walking, begging rides both in wagons and in the cars, in some way, after a number of days, I reached the city of Richmond, Virginia, about eighty-two miles from Hampton. When I reached there, tired, hungry, and dirty, it was late in the night. I had never been in a large city, and this rather added to my misery. When I reached Richmond, I was completely out of money. I had not a single acquaintance in the place, and, being unused to city ways, I did not know where to go. I applied at several places for lodging, but they all wanted money, and that was what I did not have. Knowing nothing else better to do, I walked the streets. In doing this I passed by many foodstands where fried chicken and half-moon apple pies were piled high and made to present a most tempting appearance. At that time it seemed to me that I would have promised all that I expected to possess in the future to have gotten hold of one of those chicken legs or one of those pies. But I could not get either of these, nor anything else to eat.

I must have walked the streets till after midnight. At last I became so exhausted that I could walk no longer. I was tired, I was hungry, I was everything but discouraged. Just about the time when I reached extreme physical exhaustion, I came upon a portion of a street where the board sidewalk was considerably elevated. I waited for a few minutes, till I was sure that no passers-by could see me, and then crept under the sidewalk and lay for the night upon the ground, with my satchel of clothing for a pillow. (48-49)

Both men go on to describe their gradual rise to social prominence and focus on their endeavors in behalf of others, Franklin with his social projects for Philadelphia and the nation, Washington with his program for Negro betterment.

Even this brief summary of parallels is sufficient to rearticulate the fundamental ethos behind the Horatio Alger myth, whether black or white. This hero is an economic materialist, an industrious, self-made businessman who views the world as material to be conquered in his rise to success. He is a public man, a man of action whose sense of identity and self-fulfillment derive from his social useful-ness. He is a virtuous man who upholds middle-class mores and morals. The ethos of Washington's life journey mirrors the predominant ethos of the time; therein lies its power and its influence. *Up From Slavery* is a businessman's au-tobiography, which is one reason why it met such success in the United States and abroad at a time when business was becoming big business and when the Horatio Alger myth itself was extremely popular, embodied as it was in current fiction and such autobiographies as that of Andrew Car-negie. But it met with success primarily because Washing-ton responded as a businessman would to the social climate of the late nineteenth century—a time when the black American was being systematically deprived of political and civil rights—by adopting a pragmatic stance that mirrored the white attitudinal climate. The exuberant hope of post-war Reconstruction had been shattered; a more realistic hope, deriving from a program of self-help, of assimilation into and accommodation with the dominant culture, re-placed it.

The situations that Washington and Franklin describe above, however, are only almost identical, and the differ-ences that lie in the "almost" embody the essential disparity between the white and black versions of the journey of the Horatio Alger hero. Franklin had some money and his good clothes were being sent to him; Washington had neither. Franklin could give food away; Washington could buy none at all. Franklin did not worry about lodging; Washington could find none but the space beneath the boardwalk. The obstacles along the black Horatio Alger's way, whether social, economic, or political, radically limit the fluidity of his movement in American society. They are literally antagonistic and potentially destructive. Neverthe-less, through a strict moral rectitude, Washington does manage to transform even this radical difference from a liability into an asset:

> With few exceptions, the Negro youth must work hard-er and must perform his task even better than a white youth in order to secure recognition. But out of the hard and unusual struggle which he is compelled to pass, he gets a strength, a confidence, that one misses whose pathway is comparatively smooth by reason of birth and race. (40)

In the end, Washington's optimism and faith in the sys-tem are reaffirmed in his appropriation of an autobio-graphical form that embodies the traditional American myth of social success. *Up From Slavery,* articulated in the formal language of the dominant culture, serves as a vehicle for discussing a philosophy acceptable to the dominant culture and for dramatizing, to both blacks and whites, the success of that philosophy.

II

There is yet another sharp difference between Washington's autobiographical life and the prototypical life of the Horatio Alger hero, whether Franklin's or certain later black autobiographer's. This difference is made clear in the following passage:

> In order to be successful in any kind of undertaking, I think the main thing is for one to grow to the point where he completely forgets himself; that is, to lose

himself in a great cause. In proportion as one loses
himself in this way, in the same degree does he get the
highest happiness out of his work. (181)

The fundamental paradox of Christian invisibility—that in
order to find oneself, one must lose oneself—apparently
controls Washington's drama of selfhood. Life becomes a
journey of self-sacrifice and self-effacement, characterized
by the sublimation of selfish desires in the embracement of
social causes. Fame and fortune are merely the results—not
the primary goals—of Washington's exemplary life of self-
sacrifice, which finds fruition in the improvement of the
conditions of his race. In this respect, Washington's autobiography contrasts with Franklin's and the rise of the
traditional Horatio Alger hero: there is no such tendency to
self-effacement in Franklin's narrative. Franklin's cause is
his own, although after he gains success he devotes himself
to public betterment.

The point is that there are complexities in the situation of
the black American that Franklin did not have to be self-
conscious about. The slave narrator testified to the self-
destruction consequent upon any expression of self-
assertion, whether real or imagined, whether conspicuous
or inconspicuous, which made it necessary for him to fabri-
cate a mask in order to survive. The Civil War did not end
the need for the mask because it did not end imprisonment.
Washington was a child of a Reconstruction that promised
much in the way of freedom but delivered little, if anything,
in fact. He, too, had to survive—in life as well as in autobiography. And one prerequisite was successfully met by
means of the mask of Christian invisibility; for one of the
"obstacles" Washington had to overcome was his audience.
That audience, a major determinant of Washington's approach to his life story, was, for the most part, composed

of white southerners and northerners, in contrast to the slave narrator's, which had been entirely a northern one before which he could adopt a critical attitude toward his experience in the South. Washington's approach toward his experience and that of blacks in general therefore had to be responsive to the nature of such an audience.

The first paragraphs of the autobiography establish his assumed point of view. Bitterness and vindictiveness are nonexistent; Christian love and forgiveness prevail. Of his father, a white man, he says: "But I do not find especial fault with him. He was simply another unfortunate victim of the institution which the Nation unhappily had engrafted upon it at that time" (3). He avoids retributive judgment, emphasizes "understanding." Thus, he comments about the South as a region:

I have long since ceased to cherish any spirit of bitterness against the Southern white people on account of the enslavement of my race. No one section of our country was wholly responsible for its introduction, and, besides, it was recognized and protected for years by the General Government. Having once got its tentacles fastened on to the economic and social life of the Republic, it was no easy matter for the country to relieve itself of the institution. (16)

Because the system is to blame, no one is accountable. Circumspect in order not to antagonize his white audience, Washington touches only peripherally on the brutal realities of life for the black American. He devotes the last three paragraphs of chapter 4 to these realities, concluding once again by exonerating white complicity.

I have referred to this unpleasant part of the history of

the South simply for the purpose of calling attention to
the great change that has taken place since the days of
the "Ku Klux." Today there are no such organizations
in the South, and the fact that such ever existed is
almost forgotten by both races. There are few places in
the South now where public sentiment would permit
such organizations to exist. (71)

In his avid tendency to extol the efforts of whites, especially southern whites, he is the epitome of the loving,
charitable Christian. His mask assures his survival in the
South. But it does more. It is central to Washington's role as
a black leader, functioning as a shrewd business means to
achieve his ends, a tactic earlier employed by the slave who
was often successful in avoiding work, getting food, pulling
easy jobs, if he knew how to manipulate the mask of the
"darky" effectively. It was good business to assure southerners that they were fine people, that everything was
improving, that the South was the place where the Negroes
should "cast down [their] buckets." In this way, too,
Washington could lead members of his own race as well as
whites. He described, for example, his practice at Tuskegee
of asking students and faculty for suggestions and criti-
cisms. His motivation is preeminently practical:

Few things help an individual more than to place responsibility upon him, and to let him know that you
trust him. . . . Every individual responds to confidence,
and this is not more true of any race than of the Negroes. Let them once understand that you are unselfishly interested in them, and you can lead them to any
extent. (172)

Washington's choice of the word "lead" is illuminating, for

he implies an intimate relationship between the ability to play the benign, "humble" role—"Let[ting] them . . . understand that you are unselfishly interested in them"—and the ability to lead others successfully. Such a role is extremely useful to a leader and to a con man.

Leadership, of course, implies power over those led. Washington's consciousness of and pride in such power, betrayed in his propensity for inserting in the text of the autobiography newspaper reviews praising him for a speech or other accomplishment, belie the self-effacement of the mask of Christian invisibility. One such review reads: "All the speeches were enthusiastically received, but the colored man carried off the oratorical honors, and the applause which broke out when he had finished was vociferous and long-continued" (302). In his description of the acceptance speech he made when Harvard awarded him an honorary degree in 1896, he does not include one, but four, reviews; in his description of his University of Chicago speech, he refers to the praise he received from President McKinley:

> The part of the speech which seemed to arouse the wildest and most sensational enthusiasm was that in which I thanked the President for his recognition of the Negro in his appointments during the Spanish-American war. The President was sitting in a box at the right of the stage. When I addressed him I turned toward the box, and as I finished the sentence thanking him for his generosity, the whole audience rose and cheered again and again, waving handkerchiefs and hats and canes, until the President arose in the box and bowed his acknowledgements. At that the enthusiasm broke out again, and the demonstration was almost indescribable. (255)

This passsage suggests the manipulative quality of Washington's flattering and deferential mask.

Ultimately, the mask of Christian invisibility is a means to triumph over and manipulate others. Washington's mentor General Samuel C. Armstrong had advised him "that great men cultivate love, and that only little men cherish a spirit of hatred" (165). His use of the word "cultivate," whether it is his own choice or whether he remembers the exact words of General Armstrong (the act of memory is itself revealing) implies, like the use of "lead," a self-conscious rather than a selfless response. Washington "cultivated" love as one cultivates a pose or fabricates a mask and, in so doing, gained control over others—both black and white.

The moral ambiguity inherent in Washington's use of the mask will concern certain writers of later generations such as Ralph Ellison, who explores such ambiguity in his novel *Invisible Man* when he reincarnates Washington as Dr. Bledsoe, the sycophantic southern educator who "cultivates" the mask of humility in order to manipulate white men.[6] The protagonist recalls that "he was the only one of us whom I knew—except perhaps a barber or a nursemaid—who could touch a white man with impunity."[7] The privilege of touch symbolizes Bledsoe's real power and authority over the white man: his ostensible mask of self-abnegating humility conceals a covetous ego whose self-fulfillment derives from oblique mastery. This power he reveals to the protagonist as he expels him from the college:

> "I's big and black and I say 'Yes, suh' as loudly as any burr-head when it's convenient, but I'm still the king down here. I don't care how much it appears otherwise. Power doesn't have to show off. Power is confident, self-assuring, self-starting and self-stopping, self-warming and self-justifying. When you have it,

you know it. Let the Negroes snicker and the crackers laugh! Those are the facts, son. The only ones I even pretend to please are *big* white folk, and even those I control more than they control me. This is a power set-up, son, and I'm at the controls."[8]

In order to maintain such control, Bledsoe must sacrifice the naive youth who has threatened his power structure; in other words, he must betray his own community. A leader may thus become more a tyrant than a savior, more a jailor than a liberator, a possibility W.E.B. DuBois recognized clearly when he chose to criticize Washington's program and his influence.

From another point of view, the leader may himself be the imprisoned victim, for the mask may be a form of oppression that forces the black self to deny its authentic impulses, a negative possibility apparent in the slave narratives. For the slave, the mask, a necessity for survival, could not be freely chosen. So, too, Washington, in order to be successful, must sacrifice himself to his social mask, a victimization that certainly limits his narrative art and may have limited him as a person. Not only is he not free to choose his mask; he is not free to examine that mask consciously in his autobiography. Thus, the self-portrait that emerges from the passage above describing his entry into Richmond lacks the self-parody of Franklin's portrait of himself. Unlike Franklin who was a master of the pose, Washington is mastered by the pose since it is a necessary response to his audience. And because he is not really free to control his material by maintaining a conscious distance between himself as autobiographer and himself as protagonist, his narrative is literal, unironic, unreflective.

Franklin, in contrast, was free to choose his pose, a freedom reflected in his description of the entry into Philadelphia and in subsequent descriptions of his early experimentation with various poses until he finally chose the one that would serve him best—the "plain dress" of "Benjamin Franklin of Philadelphia, Printer"—but a freedom reflected finally in the ironic distance which allows him, for example, to articulate and reexamine the advantages of his chosen pose:

> I took care not only to be in *reality* industrious and frugal, but to avoid all *appearances* of the contrary. I dressed plain and was seen at no places of idle diversion . . . and to show that I was not above my business, I sometimes brought home the paper I purchased at the stores thro' the streets on a wheelbarrow.[9]

In recreating his past life, Franklin achieves sophisticated control of his narrative by remaining outside his materials and maintaining a distance between himself as autobiographer and his younger self as protagonist. Washington does not or cannot and so is forced to narrate a two-dimensional tale of the facts of his education and his work, not a self-conscious or self-analytical (three-dimensional) tale of the choice of a mask, for the black self-assertion his mask of Christian invisibility conceals must remain concealed if he is to be successful. From this point of view, Washington is ultimately imprisoned in his social identity.

This imprisonment can be pushed further (but I want to emphasize that I am merely hypothesizing a possibility). At perhaps the most subconscious level operating to control Washington's autobiographical act and, more broadly, his political program lies a rejection of his black identity and heritage. Washington may be imprisoned in his own self-hatred, an internalization of racial hatred. His aspiration to rise above his origins to preeminence and leadership can be read on one level as the aspiration to rise above the stigma of race: his choice of the name "Washington" assumes this, for Washington is the quintessential white historical leader, the first great white father. Washington's flight is a flight toward whiteness, away from blackness. Moreover, his espousal of the ethos of the time, his economic materialism and Puritan morality, is an embracement of the white cultural life-style and a rejection of the black cultural tradition. The pride manifest in Washington's narrative is the pride of having risen above the mass of black people: he is different; he is better; he is white-like. His formal writing style, his appropriation of a traditional white literary form, is one way of saying to the white world that he is an uncommon, not a common, black.[10] This is one of the most devastating results of the black American experience—the flight of the black toward whiteness and away from blackness.[11]

III

Washington's *Up From Slavery* is central to a discussion of black American autobiography in two ways. First, since Washington is a black Horatio Alger, his narrative is representative of the pattern of autobiography that finds its public and private motivations in the individual's need to reaffirm his successful achievement of place in American society and its corollary sense of freedom. Such autobiographies are narratives of social callings, the stories of public personalities—athletes, entertainers, teachers, political leaders. Their titles alone suggest the meanings of the pattern imposed by the narrators. A large number name the personality whose life narrative is being told: *Lena* (Lena Horne), *The Joe Louis Story*, *The Archie Moore Story*, *The Raw Pearl* (Pearl Bailey). That the name has become publicly respected signals success: the name itself symbolizes a viable form of freedom. Another group of titles name the sphere in which public fame has been won: *The Fastest Bicycle Rider in the World* (Marshall W. "Major" Taylor), *Black Wings* (Lieutenant William J. Powell), *Father of the Blues* (W.C. Handy), *Born to Play Ball* (Willie Mays), *Breakthrough to the Big League* (Jackie Robinson). A third group suggests the direction of the personal journey—up, out, away, from the onus of racial handicap: *Movin' On Up* (Mahalia Jackson), *I Always Wanted to Be Somebody* (Althea Gibson), *Victory Over Myself* (Floyd Patterson), *Bursting Bonds* (William Pickens), and *Up From Slavery* itself.

There is, of course, a risk in forcing all these titles, and autobiographies, together as representative of a structural pattern in black American autobiography. In doing so, I do not mean to minimize the importance of the individual achievements nor to question the centrality of this tradition in the black experience. Like the slave narrators before them, these autobiographers have struggled for their freedom against overwhelming odds. Writing about that struggle is certainly a way of assessing the nature and cost of success as well as a way of reaffirming it. These autobiographers too enact a "rite of coherence"[12] upon the chaos of their lives. Their autobiographies are thus characterized by the prototypal motifs already elaborated in the first chapter, for example, the quest after wholeness and authenticity, the moments of disillusionment. Moreover, like the slave narrators before them, these autobiographers, rebels in their own way, are making public and political statements about the ability of the black American to achieve greatness. They are cultural heroes and heroines whose narratives are examples of the possibility of success within American society.

But a cruel irony lies at the center of Washington's "success story." In the end, he achieved his powerful place only through the acrobatics of the mask of Christian invisibility. And so his life story implies the second major pattern in black autobiography, the bleaker vision, which focuses on the self's inability to achieve a "place" in American society. Imprisoned within either black or white society or both, the individual is shackled to the chains of a socially imposed identity. Hence, his life is characterized by profound loneliness and alienation from society or possibly even from self. Finally, unwilling to wear the necessary mask, he becomes a rebel who, like the slave narrator in his first avatar as slave, breaks defiantly with society and its exacting price of self-sacrifice, to search once again for the freedom of authenticity. The conclusion of this second pattern of autobiography is characterized by a symbolic death and/or rebirth—perhaps the geographical flight from an old way of life, or disillusionment, or acceptance and thus transcendence of past experience, or an actual rebirth into a new identity.

Notes

[1]J. Saunders Redding, *No Day of Triumph,* p. 47.

[2]John Hope Franklin, ed., *Three Negro Classics,* p. xi.

[3]Emmett J. Scott and Lyman Beecher Stowe, *Booker T. Washington: Builder of a Civilization,* p. 264. Between 1901 and 1917, 110,000 copies were sold, and the book was translated into French, Spanish, German, Hindustani, and braille.

[4]Booker T. Washington, *Up From Slavery,* p. 32. Further citations will appear in the text.

[5]Benjamin Franklin, *The Autobiography of Benjamin Franklin, A Restoration of a "Fair Copy" by Max Farrand* (Berkeley: University of California Press, 1949), pp. 30-31.

[6]Ralph Ellison's *Invisible Man,* although a novel, proved invaluable in this study because it explores in a fictional autobiography

so many of the central structural and thematic motifs that concerned me here.

[7]Ellison, *Invisible Man*, p. 89.

[8]Ibid., p. 109-110.

[9]Franklin, *Autobiography*, p. 32.

[10]Rebecca Chalmers Barton, *Witnesses for Freedom*, pp. 22-23.

[11]Of course, this hypothetical possibility can be suggested because of the narrow line Washington was forced to walk between the blacks and whites in his audience. If he had been free to be totally honest we might not assume so much—nor so little.

3

FLIGHT AGAIN

There was the yearning for identification loosed in me by the sight of a solitary ant carrying a burden upon a mysterious journey.
—Richard Wright, Black Boy

The slave narratives define three dominant responses of the black slave to his environment that were to continue after slavery was officially abolished—conciliation, apparent acquiescence facilitated by conscious masking, and rebellion.[1] The young protagonist of Richard Wright's Black Boy, *growing up in the South in the first decades of the twentieth century, where disenfranchisement, segregation, and racial subordination formed the bases for continued existence, must choose among these alternatives. His impulse is to rebel openly, but to do so is to risk death. Yet he recognizes an even greater risk than death: to accept—or even appear to accept —the self-denial the South demanded of him was to invite psychological suicide. Richard, who finds it impossible to accept or to mask his rebellion against this fate, ultimately chooses open rebellion. Thus, for Wright the autobiographer, warfare—between his essential self and his environment—becomes the basic metaphor for depicting his struggle from childhood innocence to self-awareness.*

Although the autobiographies of both Washington and Wright

are narratives about southern black American experience, the pat-
terns imposed upon that experience form sharply contrasting por-
traits of self-expression. Washington traces the journey of the self
from alienation into social acceptance and prominence within
southern society: Wright traces the movement of the self further and
further into alienation from society, black and white, until flight to
the North becomes imperative. If Washington is representative of
the self finding expression through the mask of Christian love,
Wright is the opposite, refusing any mask and thereby finding
self-expression only through warfare and violence. If Washington
finds self-fulfillment through ostensibly sacrificing his own indi-
vidual concerns for the sake of the community, Wright defies
violently the community that refuses to allow his self-assertion. The
violence of the autobiography reflects the violence of the confronta-
tion between the self seeking autonomy and the society that refuses to
allow it. Whereas Washington reflects the slave narrator's desire
for a future of personal and social betterment, Wright reflects the
slave's needs for rebellion. Wright redirects our attention away
from hope back toward the violent confrontations so prominent in
the slave narrative.

   The theme of violent self-expression, in which manhood is predi-
cated on resistance to society and in which the individual's violent
self is a product of violence directed to that self by society, is
prominent in the slave narrative. Douglass, as we have observed,
narrates the incident that became the turning point of his life, the
moment in which he chose to fight back rather than suffer degrada-
tion at the hands of the overseer Covey. This moment of violent
self-assertion precipitated a strong sense of manliness. He was,
however, more fortunate than many others: he lived to write about
it.

I

Black Boy opens with a primal scene from Wright's childhood which dramatizes the complex nature of young Richard's struggle with his environment.

One winter morning in the long-ago, four-year-old days of my life I found myself standing before a fireplace, warming my hands over a mound of glowing coals, listening to the wind whistle past the house outside. All morning my mother had been scolding me, telling me to keep still, warning me that I must make no noise. And I was angry, fretful, and impatient. In the next room Granny lay ill and under the day and night care of a doctor and I knew that I would be punished if I did not obey. I crossed restlessly to the window and pushed back the long fluffy white curtains—which I had been forbidden to touch—and looked yearningly out into the empty street. I was dreaming of running and playing and shouting, but the vivid image of Granny's old, white, wrinkled, grim face, framed by a halo of tumbling black hair, lying upon a huge feather pillow, made me afraid.[2]

Bored and resentful, Richard seeks amusement, finding it in watching straws burn in the fire. His brother warns him to stop, but,

My idea was growing, blooming. Now I was wondering just how the long fluffy white curtains would look if I lit a bunch of straws and held it under them. Would I try it? Sure. I pulled several straws from the broom and held them to the fire until they blazed; I rushed to the window and brought the flame in touch with the hems of the curtains. (10)

After the house catches fire, Richard, afraid of being

punished, seeks shelter beneath it. Eventually he is re-
trieved by his father who delivers him into the firm grip of
his mother. The scene which follows is prototypal of the
experience of the autobiography:

> "You almost scared us to death," my mother muttered
> as she stripped the leaves from a tree limb to prepare it
> for my back.
>
> I was lashed so hard and long that I lost conscious-
> ness. I was beaten out of my senses and later found
> myself in bed, screaming, determined to run away,
> tussling with my mother and father who were trying to
> keep me still. I was lost in a fog of fear. A doctor was
> called—I was afterwards told—and he ordered that I
> be kept abed, that I be kept quiet, that my very life
> depended upon it. My body seemed on fire and I could
> not sleep. Packs of ice were put on my forehead to keep
> down the fever. Whenever I tried to sleep I would see
> huge wobbly white bags, like the full udders of cows,
> suspended from the ceiling above me. Later, as I grew
> worse, I could see the bags in the daytime with my eyes
> open and I was gripped by the fear that they were
> going to fall and drench me with some horrible liquid.
> Day and night I begged my mother and father to take
> the bags away, pointing to them, shaking with horror
> because no one saw them but me. Exhaustion would
> make me drift toward sleep and then I would scream
> until I was wide awake again; I was afraid to sleep.
> Time finally bore me away from the dangerous bags
> and I got well. But for a long time I was chastened
> whenever I remembered that my mother had come
> close to killing me. (13)

His domestic environment oppressively denies Richard

natural means for self-expression. That the source of this deprivation should be the "old, white, wrinkled, grim face" of his grandmother is triply significant: first, the feelings of repression and fear are symbolically linked to "white"-ness; second, illness and death are linked to "white"-ness; and third, literally and metaphorically, "black" becomes "white" rendering both "colors" potentially oppressive. In Richard's experience white and black people melt together. He is actually introduced to "whites" at a relatively late stage in his childhood:

> Though I had long known that there were people called "white" people, it had never meant anything to me emotionally. I had seen white men and women upon the streets a thousand times, but they never looked particularly "white." To me they were merely people like other people, yet somehow strangely different because I had never come in close touch with any of them. For the most part I never thought of them; they simply existed somewhere in the background of the city as a whole. It might have been that my tardiness in learning to sense white people as "white" people came from the fact that many of my relatives were "white"-looking people. (30-32)

Richard, deprived of normal outlets for his creative energies—running, playing, shouting—seeks an alternative form of self-affirmation. His imaginative curiosity combines with his childhood frustration to find another outlet, the destructive act of burning the curtains he has been forbidden to touch. Putting the torch to them is a means of acting out his rebellion against his oppressive, deathly domestic environment. This act of domestic rebellion is the symbolic precursor of his larger social rebellion, for the curtains are "fluffy, white." In addition, they cover the windows, thereby keeping out the sun, and, in this way, they symbolize the restrictions of white society which limit his vision and which he is forbidden to "touch," to challenge. The curiosity and unfocused energy that propel this primal event, when informed by knowledge and sharpened by later suffering, become the creativity of the writer, ultimately the most powerful weapon in Wright's arsenal of self-defense. Creativity and violence become the two sides of the same coin.

Since the house burns down, Richard's act of rebellion ends in total destruction of his environment, just as his later rebellion is to threaten the status quo of the larger southern environment, and from this destruction he now must and later will have to flee. At this time, however, his flight is unsuccessful. He is dragged out from under the house to suffer the wrath of his mother. Her violent reaction is a response in part to his willfulness, which threatens to be, and in this case almost is, self-destructive. The familial act of love is an act of violence: his mother, desiring to protect him from future disaster, almost kills him. Richard's delirious vision incorporates all these significances in its symbolism. The "huge wobbly white bags" (or breasts) represent his mother who has just beaten him mercilessly. They contain a horrible liquid which he fears will drench him; his mother's milk (symbolic of the family) has, so to speak, gone sour in the sense that it threatens to drown out his individuality.

Ralph Ellison describes this form of behavior in his essay on *Black Boy* entitled "Richard Wright's Blues." According to Ellison, the black family's impulse to suppress and even destroy self-assertion in the child is an impulse of distorted love. The family knows unconsciously that in order for the young boy to survive physically and psychologically in society, he must be kept from questioning it too closely and from challenging it too overtly. The family's function is dual: it is

> to protect the Negro from whirling away from the undifferentiated mass of his people into the unknown, symbolized in its most abstract form by insanity, and most concretely by lynching; and to protect him from those unknown forces within himself which might urge him to reach out for that social and human equality which the white South says he cannot have. Rather than throw himself against the charged wires of his prison, he annihilates the impulses within him.[3]

Throughout childhood, the family's protective instincts continue to terrify the youth, who nevertheless challenges them repeatedly. In response, the family resorts to beatings which Richard then refuses to suffer silently because he knows them to be unjustified. They are beatings that indicate just how distorted familial responses become when exposed to the relentless forces of racism: their intent is protection, their manner violence, their result destruction of personality. As Ellison observes:

> *Black Boy* . . . illustrates that this personal quality, shaped by outer violence and inner fear, is ambivalent. Personal warmth is accompanied by an equally personal coldness, kindliness by cruelty, regard by malice. And these opposites are as quickly set off against the member who gestures toward individuality as a lynch mob forms at the cry of rape.[4]

Richard's violent encounters with his family are microcosmic reflections of his violent encounters with society at large. The white bags simultaneously symbolize white society, which, in response to his act of rebellion, seeks to drown him in the terrible liquid of nonentity and thereby wash away his imagination and individuality. Later, after his uncle is killed by a white mob, Richard, his mother, and aunt must flee secretly at night. Wright explains:

> Uncle Hoskins had simply been plucked from our midst and we, figuratively, had fallen on our faces to avoid looking into that white-hot face of terror that we knew loomed somewhere above us. This was as close as white terror had ever come to me and my mind reeled. Why had we not fought back, I asked my mother, and the fear that was in her made her slap me into silence. (64)

The "white-hot face" echoes the "white bags." His reaction to both is terror and fear and a subsequent need to rebel against both white and black society. Significantly, his mother slaps him out of fear when he asks why they had not fought back. Fear-violence-counterviolence is an established pattern of behavior in Richard's life. His world becomes a cosmos of violence and repressive love as the black and white communities combine to demand a denial of self to which he cannot submit, against which he must rebel.

II

Richard, like the slave narrator, is imprisoned by the exigencies of survival in southern society. Moreover, like the slave narrator, he is alone, a virtual orphan who must discover his own way to the "promised land" of self-actualization, for first his father and eventually his mother desert him. Early memories of his father, like the other early memories, abound in repression and violence: "He became important and forbidding to me only when I learned that I could not make noise when he was asleep in the daytime. He was the lawgiver in our family and I never laughed in his presence. . . . He was always a stranger to me, always somehow alien and remote" (16-17). As lawgiver, Richard's father becomes the oppressor who controls rather than guides; and just as the slave narrator had defied the slavemaster, so Richard must rebel. When he and his brother bring home a stray cat, his father's response is emotionally violent: "Kill that damn thing! . . . Do anything, but get it away from here!" Richard does precisely this. When his mother reports this to his father, Richard taunts him: "You told me to kill 'im." In this way, Richard defies his father's power and authority and thus triumphs over him. When soon after, his father leaves and hunger becomes a way of life, Richard's concepts of "father" and "hunger" merge: "As the days slid past the image of my father became associated with my pangs of hunger, and whenever I felt hunger I thought of him with a deep biological bitterness" (21).

Paradoxically, it is Richard's mother who temporarily becomes his guide, teaching him the necessary lesson of self-defense when she refuses to protect him from a gang of youths who, having once succeeded in stealing his grocery money, await him again:

> She slammed the door and I heard the key turn in the lock. I shook with fright. I was alone upon the dark, hostile streets and gangs were after me. I had the choice of being beaten at home or away from home. I clutched the stick, crying, trying to reason. If I were beaten at home, there was absolutely nothing that I could do about it; but if I were beaten in the streets, I had a chance to fight and defend myself. I walked

slowly down the sidewalk, coming closer to the gang of boys, holding the stick tightly, I was so full of fear that I could scarcely breathe. I was almost upon them now.

"There he is again!" the cry went up.

They surrounded me quickly and began to grab for my hand.

"I'll kill you!" I threatened. (24-25)

Superficially, this act seems to contradict her earlier violent response to his self-assertion. In the earlier instance, she, as a representative of the community, punishes him for this violent self-assertiveness; in the latter instance, she forces him to respond violently toward others. But actually both these lessons are lessons in self-defense. The first is a lesson that is necessary for survival in white society, the second, a lesson necessary for survival in black society. Richard is, at this time, literally forced to fight in order to survive on the streets. As he matures, the value of self-assertion through physical warfare will find new avenues of expression in psychological and verbal warfare.

When his mother finally succumbs to permanent illness and disability, Richard is deprived of his last familial source of strength. Her illness was to affect him profoundly:

My mother's suffering grew into a symbol in my mind, gathering to itself all the poverty, the ignorance, the helplessness; the painful, baffling, hunger-ridden days and hours; the restless moving, the futile seeking, the uncertainty, the fear, the dread; the meaningless pain and the endless suffering. Her life set the emotional tone of my life, colored the men and women I was to meet in the future, conditioned my relation to events that had not yet happened, determined my attitude to situations and circumstances I had yet to face. A somberness of spirit that I was never to lose settled over me during the slow years of my mother's unrelieved suffering, a somberness that was to make me stand apart and look upon excessive joy with suspicion, that was to make me self-conscious, that was to make me keep forever on the move, as though to escape a nameless fate seeking to overtake me. (111-112)

The older autobiographer looks back upon this loss, assigning to it in retrospect the meaning that it came to hold for his later life. For the more modern slave narrator, the dogs of the overseer still pursue, though they have assumed the qualities of a more general "fate"—one that has its origin in the bitter experience of childhood.

As a result of this bitter experience, the twelve-year-old boy forms a "conception of life": "the meaning of living came only when one was struggling to wring a meaning out of meaningless suffering" (112). This struggle is the struggle of the rebel who, because he refuses to acquiesce in the conspiracy of his black family community, a microcosm of the community at large, to force him to deny his individuality, is alienated completely from anything but his own self-consciousness. Richard recognizes that the separation he feels is deadly when, at the age of fifteen, he says of himself: "In me was shaping a yearning for a kind of consciousness, a mode of being that the way of life around me had said could not be, must not be, and upon which the penalty of death had been placed" (187).

The extent of this alienation is unexpectedly revealed when Richard overhears a conversation between Uncle Tom and his daughter, who also live in his grandmother's house. In this conversation, Uncle Tom adamantly reminds her to avoid the rebellious boy:

"Do you want me to break your neck? Didn't I tell you
to stay away from him? That boy's a dangerous fool, I
tell you! Then why don't you keep away from him?
And make the other children keep away from him! Ask
me no questions, but do as I tell you! Keep away from
him, or I'll skin you!" (191)

"How long had this been going on?" Richard asks himself.

I thought back over the time since Uncle Tom and his
family had moved into the house, and I was filled with
dismay as I recalled that on scarcely any occasion had
any of his children ever been alone with me. Be careful
now, I told myself; don't see what isn't there. . . . But no
matter how carefully I weighed my memories, I could
recall no innocent intimacy, no games, no playing,
none of the association that usually exists between
young people living in the same house. Then suddenly
I was reliving that early morning when I had held
Uncle Tom at bay with my razors. Though I must have
seemed brutal and desperate to him, I had never
thought of myself as being so, and now I was appalled
at how I was regarded. It was a flash of insight which
altered the entire course of my life. I was now definitely
decided upon leaving home. (191-192)

The realization that he is an outcast to be avoided at all costs
is the "turning point" of Richard's early life. The family sees
him as a dangerous rebel, and its instinctive behavioral
patterns demand that he be disowned since he risks his own
and the community's annihilation. His longing to be an
authentic self struggles against society's demand that he be
a "nigger." The struggle sharpens his anger toward a hos-

tile world as it taxes his inner resolve to overcome that world.

Richard shrinks from the two frequently traveled roads to survival for a black in southern society. There is the rigid, stifling religion of his grandmother, Aunt Aggie, and his mother, which encourages resignation to this world by preaching that there will be revenge enough in inheriting the next. Or, there is the masking of Griggs and Shorty which provides the limited psychological revenge of conscious deception. When Griggs warns Richard of the gravity of reacting honestly to whites, he explains and demonstrates the nature of masking:

> "You know, Dick, you may think I'm an Uncle Tom, but I'm not. I hate these white people, hate 'em with all my heart. But I can't show it; if I did, they'd kill me." He paused and looked around to see if there were any white people within hearing distance. "Once I heard an old drunk nigger say:
>
> > All these white folks dressed so fine
> > Their ass-holes smell just like mine. . . ."
>
> I laughed uneasily, looking at the white faces that passed me. But Griggs, when he laughed, covered his mouth with his hand and bent at the knees, a gesture which was unconsciously meant to conceal his excessive joy in the presence of whites. (204)

The Christian tenet of long suffering and Griggs' tactic of masking true feelings repel Richard, however much they insure survival. Religion, since it denies the self, applauds the selfless, and promises heavenly fulfillment, devalues the needs of oppressed blacks in the here-and-now and counsels them to be content with their social position. Masking also denies legitimate self-assertion since the real responses of the self must consciously be sacrificed to the mask. Sometimes it even demands self-degradation as when Shorty allows a white man to kick him in order to get twenty-five cents for lunch. Both options spell mere survival. In the one instance, a wall of other-worldliness and, in the other, a wall of disguise, protect the individual from destruction but keep him from attacking the sources of his oppression. So imprisoned, the individual is condemned to invisibility.

The curse of invisibility is to be treated as an object, a state of being symbolized by the two names "nigger" and "boy." The former is symbolic of the denial of individuality, the latter the denial of manhood. These two names function, as do the methods of survival, to keep Richard physically and psychologically in his invisible "place." They are used by white society, but, in a more immediate way, they are used by black society so that he will survive in a white society. (When his family chastises him for some breach of social action, they call him "nigger.")

Against his will, Richard temporarily succumbs to these social identities in order to survive: he lies, steals, wears the mask of fawning ingratiation. The price, of course, is a half-life. As he puts it:

> I had been what my surroundings had demanded, what my family—conforming to the dictates of the whites above them—had exacted of me, and what the whites had said that I must be. Never being fully able to be myself, I had slowly learned that the South could recognize but a part of a man. (284)

Ultimately, he chooses to reject this social mask of inferiority and invisibility and, in doing so, becomes a full-fledged rebel. Until this point, his only weapon against this stigmatizing invisibility has been violence against his immediate family rather than society at large. Now it is the "word" that will become the weapon he uses to attack society and liberate his own essential self.

III

At an early age, Richard perceives the power of words: but his experiences with them are violently punitive. There are the words learned at school and scrawled on neighborhood windows, that his mother makes him wash off. Later, after the story of *Bluebeard and His Seven Wives* elicits a "total emotional response" from him, he tries to read by himself.

> Usually I could not decipher enough words to make the story have meaning. I burned to learn to read novels and I tortured my mother into telling me the meaning of every strange word I saw, not because the word itself had any value, but because it was the gateway to a forbidden and enchanting land. (49)

Without understanding the meaning of words, Richard responds to their evocative power. Then one evening as his grandmother washes him, "words—words whose meaning I did not fully know—had slipped out of my mouth" (49). He had asked his grandmother to kiss him "back there," and for this he suffers the wrath of the entire family. Feeling no guilt, unable to comprehend why he should be punished, Richard only recognizes the effect of his words upon others, a power that fascinates him:

> The tremendous upheaval that my words had caused made me know that there lay back of them much more than I could figure out, and I resolved that in the future I would learn the meaning of why they had beat and denounced me. (53)

The courtship with words extends throughout his youth; he reads everything he can find and even tries his hand at short story writing. The successful publication of one story, however, does not gain him the praise he desires, but rather chastisement and misunderstanding. Later, he idealistically decides upon a career in writing and shares his dream with a new employer, whose reaction is significantly described as an "assault" on his ego. She asks him why he is continuing his education beyond the seventh grade; he answers that he wants to become a writer.

> "A what?" she demanded.
> "A writer," I mumbled.
> "For what?"
> "To write stories," I mumbled defensively.
> "You'll never be a writer," she said. "Who on earth put such ideas into your nigger head?"
> "Nobody," I said.
> "I didn't think anybody ever would," she declared indignantly.
> As I walked around her house to the street, I knew that I would not go back. The woman had assaulted my ego; she had assumed that she knew my place in life, what I felt, what I ought to be, and I resented it with all

my heart. Perhaps she was right; perhaps I would never be a writer; but I did not want her to say so. (162)

Writing, for a black, lay beyond the structure of socially acceptable possibilities in the South and thus is linked with self-assertion, individuality, manhood, and, by association, rebellion. Both his family's negative response to his successful attempt at short story writing and the white woman's incredulous response show a recognition of the rebellion inherent in such a dream.

Richard comes to appreciate this association fully when he reads H.L. Mencken, a decisive step in his development; he comes to recognize the militancy and potential violence of words, a violence he has already experienced emotionally but not intellectually.

That night in my rented room, while letting the hot water run over my can of pork and beans in the sink, I opened *A Book of Prefaces* and began to read. I was jarred and shocked by the style, the clear, clean, sweeping sentences. Why did he write like that? And how did one write like that? I pictured the man as a raging demon, slashing with his pen, consumed with hate, denouncing everything American, extolling everything European or German, laughing at the weaknesses of people, mocking God, authority. What was this? I stood up, trying to realize what reality lay behind the meaning of the words. . . . Yes, this man was fighting, fighting with words. He was using words as a weapon, using them as one would use a club. Could words be weapons? Well, yes, for here they were. Then, maybe, perhaps, I could use them as a weapon? (271-272)

Wright's portrait of Mencken "as a raging demon, slashing with his pen" is significant. The pen becomes the most effective weapon of warfare and, for the imagination, becomes the equivalent of physical violence. This initiation into the weaponry of words leads him on to more and more writers who awaken him to the reality of the world outside the South. He finds in writers the attitudes toward life he has harbored alone within himself.

Wright will imitate Mencken when, in his later writing, he uses the pen as weapon, the word as ammunition for protesting the life of the black American. *Native Son* itself is a weapon, "a loaded pistol at the head of the white world."[5] The theme of violent self-expression is central to structural design and meaning in this novel as it is in the autobiography. Imprisoned within his social invisibility in an oppressive society, Bigger senses that his acts of murder are the only free creative actions of his life because they involve the power to determine a fate for himself and thus, at least momentarily, the power of visibility and potency. Violent rebellion is a form of liberation:

> He had done this. He had brought all this about. In all of his life these two murders were the most meaningful things that had ever happened to him. He was living, truly and deeply, no matter what others might think looking at him with their blind eyes. Never had he had the chance to live out the consequences of his actions; never had his will been so free as in this night and day of fear and murder and flight.[6]

Since society does not sanction murder, at least theoretically, Bigger's act of violent self-assertion makes him a social outcast. In expressing his own individuality, he is forced to violate societal norms as the slave narrator had been forced to do; and, like the slave narrator, his sense of freedom and, thus, his sense of identity emanate from these very acts of criminality. Bigger mirrors the experience of his creator: violence becomes the only way through which Richard can assert his individuality. Bigger is, of course, a real murderer and must flee from the police. But Richard too has to flee, for his attitudes are murderous to the way of life in the South and subject, therefore, to prosecution.

IV

Richard cannot find self-fulfillment in the South:

> What, then, was there? I held my life in my mind, in my consciousness each day, feeling at times that I would stumble and drop it, spill it forever. My reading had created a vast sense of distance between me and the world in which I lived and tried to make a living, and that sense of distance was increasing each day. (277)

The "vast sense of distance" is the distance, finally unbearable, between his authentic self and his social identity. So he chooses to leave the South, as the slave had chosen to escape many years earlier, in hopes of finding a "place" of legitimate self-expression denied him in the South. His departure is a willed act of self-defense, "a conviction that if I did not leave I would perish, either because of possible violence of others against me, or because of my possible violence against them" (282).

The actual moment of confrontation does not arise for Wright. The real implications of his statement are better seen in the work of Ely Green, whose autobiography concludes, like Wright's, with flight. Born of a white man and a Negro woman, Ely is too light-skinned to feel close to the

black community, but he is, of course, considered a "nigger" by the white community. His early years, like Wright's,
are characterized by increasing alienation. His childhood
experience of being called "nigger" is a trauma that
prompts him to conclude: "As young as I were, it seemed to
me a Negro was just worthless. What could he be? Still a
slave?"[7] A bastard, Ely soon determines that he will be a
man, not a "nigger." But his self-assertion is challenged by
the social system: in protecting his dogs from poor whites,
he violates the codes. Mama, to assure the whites that she
has taught him to be respectful, lashes him in front of them.
To this, he reacts violently:

> I started cursing them, calling them all kinds of sons of
> bitches, and telling them that as soon as I could get a
> gun I would kill them. Jumping up and down swear-
> ing, I said: "I will never stop until I kill you. I don't want
> to live if I have to crawl to you poor white sagers."[8]

Running is the only solution: Ely leaves town quickly, having actually experienced what Wright anticipates.

Wright's autobiography is essentially a twentieth-century
version of the earlier slave narrative, explicitly and implicitly echoing its themes. Emancipation has not brought
freedom to the South even a half-century after its incep-
tion: the South remains a slave plantation where Richard is
still imprisoned in an oppressive, less-than-human social
identity. There, he is—and will ever remain—a "nigger"
and a "boy." Thus, like the slave narrator's story, Wright's
autobiography is the story of an individual willing to rebel
to the point of annihilation in order to remain inviolate.
Richard's longing for visible selfhood rather than deceptive
invisibility makes subservience to the racial norms of the
South impossible for him. He must flee to escape emascula-

tion. His running is a positive act for it is potentially redemptive, and it has direction: the North beckons with
possibility. The last pages of *Black Boy* testify to his hope,
the hope of the slave narrator before him, that a "home"
and a "better day" await him in the North.

His journey, however, is not informed by unqualified
hope. He realizes that he will always carry the South with
him, for he is its child. Nevertheless, he envisions himself as
a hopeful "experiment":

> So in leaving, I was taking a part of the South to
> transplant in alien soil, to see if it could grow differ-
> ently, if it could drink of new and cool rains, bend in
> strange winds, respond to the warmth of other suns,
> and, perhaps, to bloom. . . . And if that miracle ever
> happened, then I would know that there was yet hope
> in that southern swamp of despair and violence, that
> light could emerge even out of the blackest of the
> southern night. I would know that the South too could
> overcome its fear, its hate, its cowardice, its heritage of
> guilt and blood, its burden of anxiety and compulsive
> cruelty. (284-285)

Wright knows that he is running *away* from the South as
much as he is running *to* the North. The autobiography
does not conclude with his having achieved a new identity
but rather with his breaking away from his past and hoping
for a rebirth, a blooming into a new, more legitimate self.

V

Wright's impulse to write his autobiography was not
Washington's impulse: it was not an answer to society's
curiosity and respect. Certainly he was motivated in writing

Black Boy as in writing *Native Son,* like the slave narrator, by
a political need to expose publicly the psychic destruction of
personality resulting from America's racism: his experience is that of many a black man in America. *Black Boy,* too,
is a loaded pistol. But beyond that, judging from the tone
and intensity of his narrative, he was motivated by a pas-
sionately personal impulse—a deeply felt need in his soul to
get this experience outside of himself, to embody it and
deliver it up and out. In the act of writing *Black Boy,* Wright
journeys back into his past in search of himself. This very
process is a personal form of psychoanalysis. In distilling
the essence of his childhood coming of age in the South at
the beginning of the century, he recreates a total environment of violence and counterviolence, of too acute sensitivity, of ambivalent love, of pervasive and inescapable oppression, out of which his consciousness evolved.
Moreover, he analyzes the forces that shaped him and his
own inherent qualities that responded to those forces. Out
of this act of analysis and creativity comes further understanding, further consciousness of who he is and how he
became what he became: Richard Wright. In turn, to come
to understand is somehow to transcend the oppression of
the past, to liberate oneself from its burdensome and haunt-
ing omnipresence, if only in the momentary catharsis provided by the act of imposing order upon it.

Early in his life, Wright, driven by an acute sensitivity,
found that momentary sense of liberation through creativity. He describes how in his youth he created fantasies as a
way of experiencing a sense of power:

> Because I had no power to make things happen outside
> of me in the objective world, I made things happen
> within. Because my environment was bare and bleak, I
> endowed it with unlimited potentialities, redeemed it

for the sake of my own hungry and cloudy yearning.
(83)

In reacting to the oppressive environment against which as
a lonely individual he feels impotent, the child internalizes
that impotence, emotionally channeling it into fantasies
that the older Wright calls "moral bulwarks." The fantasies
allow him to maintain some semblance of power and masculinity while living in a world permeated with violence and
fear. Later he finds such momentary liberation, control,
will, in writing.

Lurking beneath the surface of the carefully controlled
and skillfully recreated past experience lies a persistent
anger and violence evident in the immediacy and vividness,
the engagement of the writer, the control of the material.
Such willful control echoes the ironic control of the slave
narrator, a surface manifestation of the turbulence of emotion held deep inside the escaped slave. Richard Wright
turns us back to the slave narrator who, in writing about his
experience in slavery, gave it distance and thus gained
control over it, and forward to the more contemporary
writers who find that writing about their lives can result in a
liberating experience of self-control, self-mastery, and
self-knowledge. Writing an autobiography becomes a vehicle for liberating the imprisoned self from the oppressive
burden of past experience.

VI

For the black American in the early decades of the twentieth century, the "place" of freedom eventually dwindled
away. It was no longer the entire North as it theoretically
had been for the escaping slave of the slave narrative.
Geographically, it included only certain sections of certain

cities; socially, it included only the intellectual liberal elite, and even their acceptance was suspect. Wright chose Chicago. Others, like Langston Hughes, fled to Harlem, which became a "home" for everything black during the Renaissance of the 1920s. Hughes' first autobiography, *The Big Sea,* traces the initial promise and ultimate disillusion of that home. The narrative opens with his first trip to sea at the age of twenty-one, a trip to Africa. Throwing his books overboard because, as he says, "books had been happening to me," he opts for real life rather than vicarious experience. But the climactic moment of his African trip reveals to him a grim reality. The scenery itself is everything he hoped for: "wild and lovely, the people dark and beautiful, the palm trees tall, the sun bright, and the rivers deep."[9] However, the crucial realization is forced upon him: "The Africans looked at me and would not believe I was a Negro" (11). In search of community and identity in Africa, he finds instead alienation as an American Negro. "Negro," the next chapter, flashes back, recreating his American Negro experience prior to the trip, while part II, "The Big Sea," narrates his wanderings, subsequent to his disillusionment, throughout Europe and the northern United States in search of a legitimate home. Like the slave narrator, Hughes is a running man, but with a difference—his running lacks direction.

Only momentarily does Hughes find direction as he journeys to Harlem during the 1920s. Like the slave narrator before him who had ostensibly found a community of white and black abolitionists into which he was accepted and to which he belonged, Hughes becomes a part of a community of intellectuals, both black and white, gathered together to live and help each other gain an audience. He finds a home in which his needs for self-assertion are met. He becomes visible—but only for a time. Suddenly the tenuousness of acceptance in that home surfaces ruthlessly. The white patron who has provided his livelihood in order that he might write freely and whom he trusts implicitly betrays Hughes' real invisibility:

> Great wealth had given to a woman who meant to be kind the means to power, and a technique of power, of so mighty a strength that I do not believe she herself knew what that force might become. She possessed the power to control people's lives—pick them up and put them down when and where she wished.
>
> She wanted me to be primitive and know and feel the intuitions of the primitive. But, unfortunately, I did not feel the rhythms of the primitive surging through me, and so I could not live and write as though I did. I was only an American Negro—who had loved the surface of Africa and the rhythms of Africa—but I was not African. I was Chicago and Kansas City and Broadway and Harlem. And I was not what she wanted me to be. So, in the end it all came back very near to the old impasse of white and Negro again, white and Negro —as do most relationships in America. (324-325)

The autobiography turns full circle on itself. Hughes introduces his life story when he finds he is not accepted in Africa; now he discovers America will accept him only as an African primitive. Even here in the liberal milieu of Harlem, freedom is a chimera, for all of American society is incapable of accepting anything but a mask. The paradox inherent in Frederick Douglass' chastisement for not sounding enough like an illiterate slave presaged the paradoxical nature of the Harlem Renaissance itself. Because white patronage and support made it possible, the white audience often dictated the black literary themes.

These themes, in turn, reflected the projected identity that audience demanded of the black American.

The Renaissance ended with the depression; so does the autobiography:

> That spring for me (and, I guess, all of us) was the end of the Harlem Renaissance. We were no longer in vogue, anyway, we Negroes. Sophisticated New Yorkers turned to Noel Coward. Colored actors began to go hungry, publishers politely rejected new manuscripts, and patrons found other uses for their money. The cycle that had charlestoned into being on the dancing heels of *Shuffle Along* now ended in *Green Pastures* with De Lawd. (334)

Hughes concludes with the loss of any illusions of finding a home in America, a spiritual disillusionment that finds symbolic expression in his physical breakdown. And yet, the disillusioning recognition of invisibility, though painful, is a form of escape to a more authentic freedom, for Hughes is no longer imprisoned in the illusion that he is a visible man. It may not be the freedom he longed for; it is, however, a real alternative, an alternative that confronts Richard Wright also; for, in fact, Wright's book is only two-thirds the original length of the manuscript.[10] The last third traces Wright's years in Chicago and his experience with the Communist party, years culminating in complete disillusionment with the "promised land." The reality of Wright's experience after his flight North, like that of Hughes, proves those earlier dreams and hopes of acceptance and self-fulfillment in a new social milieu to be merely pipe dreams.

No "place" in America is free for them: all America is the

"South" of the slave narrative, imprisoning the black American in a socially determined identity, disallowing any legitimate self-assertion. Total alienation becomes the only way of life that allows no illusions of visibility. To escape the stereotypes of his projected social identity, the black must escape America altogether. So, as William Wells Brown finally did eighty years earlier, Wright and Hughes expatriate to Europe and the world at large. The black American, free of illusions of visibility within American society, can only continue his flight onward.

This pattern of ceaseless wandering is dramatized in Hughes' second autobiography, *I Wonder as I Wander,* and Claude McKay's autobiography, *A Long Way from Home.* "All my life," McKay concludes, "I have been a troubadour wanderer."[11] Ultimately, the wanderer is a lonely man whose exile is ambiguous. On the one hand, it is potentially negative. With no geographical place of freedom, the exile may be forever plagued with a lack of at-home-ness. Such total alienation is a devastating burden. Or he may, in fact, be running from himself and his past. Either way, the act of running becomes a new form of imprisonment. On the other hand, exile can be positive if it becomes the means to freedom and not an end in itself. The alternative to geographical freedom becomes the discovery of spiritual freedom. The ultimate place of freedom lies within the self, which alone must be content to create its own "free" consciousness.

Notes

[1]Charles H. Nichols, *Many Thousand Gone,* p. 73.
[2]Richard Wright, *Black Boy,* p. 9. Further citations will appear in the text.

³Ralph Ellison, "Richard Wright's Blues," *Shadow and Act,* pp. 89-90.

⁴Ibid., p. 90.

⁵Charles I. Glickberg, "Negro Fiction in America," p. 482.

⁶Richard Wright, *Native Son,* pp. 225-26.

⁷Ely Green, *Ely,* p. 22.

⁸Ibid., p. 224.

⁹Langston Hughes, *The Big Sea,* p. 11. Further citations will appear in the text.

¹⁰See Constance Webb, *Richard Wright: A Biography,* pp. 207-208, for probable reasons.

¹¹Claude McKay, *A Long Way from Home,* p. 354.

4

CONVERSIONS

"You start Saul, and end up Paul," my grandfather often said.

—Ralph Ellison, Invisible Man

The "invisible man" of Ralph Ellison's novel has found his freedom totally alienated as he ultimately is, in the expatriated world of an underground hole. Earlier in the expressionistic hospital episode, the young protagonist has been clamped into a machine, his head "encircled by a piece of cold metal like the iron cap worn by the occupant of an electric chair."[1] The doctors examining him demand, "Who . . . are . . . you?" and although he strains to remember, he cannot. Left alone, he struggles first to answer and finally, frustrated by his inability to answer, struggles to free himself from the machine:

> *I fell to plotting ways of short-circuiting the machine. Perhaps if I shifted my body about so that the two nodes would come together—No, not only was there no room but it might electrocute me. I shuddered. Whoever else I was, I was no Samson. I had no desire to destroy myself even if it destroyed the machine; I wanted freedom, not destruction. It was exhausting, for no matter what the scheme I conceived, there was one constant*

flaw—myself. There was no getting around it. I could no more escape than I could think of my identity. Perhaps, I thought, the two things are involved with each other. When I discover who I am, I'll be free. [*Emphasis mine.*] *(184)*

The protagonist is unable to answer precisely because he does not know who he is: he has always accepted the identity given him on a slip of paper by society. In his interview with the Paris Review after publication, Ellison commented explicitly on the significance of these socially determined identities. "Each section," claims Ellison, "begins with a sheet of paper; each piece of paper is exchanged for another and contains a definition of his identity, or the social role he is to play as defined for him by others. But all say essentially the same thing. 'Keep this nigger boy running.' "[2]

Indeed, "this nigger boy" has been kept running by coercion in a series of experiences repetitive in nature, but various in ambience, which culminate in a cataclysmic Harlem riot during which he stumbles into the unilluminated sewer hole, there ironically to find illumination. The nature of that illumination is the perception of his real identity: "invisible man." Stripped of any illusions of visibility, the protagonist, because he has found his name, because that name is his identity, is "free." And so, he burns the papers, those old illusory identities, for "once he recognizes the hole of darkness into which these papers put him, he has to burn them."[3] The fire from this rite is symbolic of his illumination—an illumination further symbolized in the literal description of his underground land the ceiling of which is decorated with 1,369 light bulbs, all ablaze. "Light confirms my reality, gives birth to my form" (5), he declares in the prologue. As his boomeranging experiences validate, conscious acknowledgment of his real invisibility is his freedom: "I myself, after existing some twenty years, did not become alive until I discovered my invisibility" (6). Life is form, form identity, identity freedom. But such freedom is won at the cost of human *community—the invisible man is an expatriate from society alone in an underground hideout—for society's dues of self-sacrifice are ineluctable. The invisible man's oneiric vision of total and bloody emasculation confirms this axiomatic truth only too vividly. The invisibility that catapulted the escaped slave from the South to the North and sometimes from the North to England, that catapulted Richard Wright and Langston Hughes to Europe and Africa, catapults Ellison's protagonist into the sewer hole.*

Ellison's Invisible Man *is itself a kind of critical exploration of the patterns of selfhood in black American autobiography, a fictional slave narrative that recapitulates the various avatars of the black self in his quest after a free identity up to the 1940s and presages the complex developments in black autobiography after that. As a prospective Booker T. Washington, the naive protagonist begins his quest for identity with a scholarship to "Tuskegee." Washington, as I noted earlier, is reincarnated as Dr. Bledsoe, the powerful southern educator who cultivates the mask of humility in order to manipulate others, black and white. Because the naive youth has threatened the equilibrium of Bledsoe's power structure, he is sent running North, a movement that recalls the flight of Richard Wright. Both men run North with the hope of future betterment; Richard, however, unlike Ellison's naif who is coerced into running, does so because he can no longer sacrifice his authentic impulses to the social identity demanded of him. In fact, Richard is no naif; he is only too self-conscious of his imprisoning role. Violence, characteristic of Richard's confrontations with society, erupts again and again in* Invisible Man, *here as in* Black Boy, *pitting black against black—the boxing match, the Golden Day mayhem, the paint factory explosion, and finally the riot. The intense pressure of the stereotype is immitigable. The resultant destruction, abetted by both black and white society, is of the authentic self: the invisible man is, ultimately, only a black sambo doll controlled by society's strings. For although Ellison's youthful pro-*

tagonist does realize his dream of becoming another leader when he joins the Brotherhood, he, unlike Dr. Bledsoe who controls in his leadership, is a pawn in the Brotherhood's game of power.

The youth's belief in his visibility is the illusion that is finally and violently destroyed during the destruction of the riot. This disillusion is precisely what befalls Langston Hughes when he finds that he has merely been a reflection of his white patron's fantasies of the black poet. Moreover, the invisible man's febrile narrative is redolent of that "nausea" that results from Hughes' sudden recognition of invisibility, his physical reaction mirroring his spiritual recoil. The underground sojourn is a figurative image of Hughes' nervous breakdown, a state from which he can review his experience and find some kind of release in the mere recognition of his lack of freedom. The ex-slave could escape this slavery, but the contemporary slave can escape it perhaps only by going underground and escaping American society altogether in a life of expatriation.

And yet, there is another possibility—embodied within Ellison's characterization of Ras the Exhorter, the black nationalist. Although the invisible man (and Ellison himself) ultimately characterizes Ras as a destructive agent (Ras the Destroyer) who, like Dr. Bledsoe and Lucius Brockway, fights in the end not against the white community but against other blacks, he gives Ras some of the most compelling speeches in the novel. By the time Ellison wrote, the black nationalist movement, manifested in various forms, had already had a long history, stretching back into the nineteenth century and the early twentieth with Marcus Garvey's Back-to-Africa movement. Then in the late 1950s and early 1960s it exploded upon the American scene as the Black Muslim movement. Espousing black pride and solidarity, black nationalism calls for separation from, not assimilation into, the currupt white community. The authentic black self unites with other black selves to form a new community led by the "black" leader, a militant attacker who rejects the long tradition of emasculated leadership. This is a new

*and significantly changed version of the black man's traditional
attempt to find authentic selfhood in some social role. If Booker T.
Washington's* Up From Slavery *chronicles an earlier phase of the
black leader's drama of selfhood,* The Autobiography of Malcolm X *chronicles its recent phase, though this phase too has its
predecessors in Frederick Douglass'* My Bondage and My
Freedom *and W.E.B. DuBois* Dusk of Dawn.

*Ellison's insights in this case are prophetic even though he
personally has little sympathy for any kind of public identity. Ras's
name is symbolic of his public identity as a black nationalist leader;
he is an "exhorter" spewing forth his wrath upon the white man.
Malcolm Little's "X" is similarly symbolic of his vision of his public
identity in American society, and he, like Ras, spews forth wrath.
This "X" is not, however, the only name he bears in his autobiography. His first identity is Malcolm Little, alias "nigger," his final,
El Hajj Malik El-Shabazz. The story of these names is the story of
his life, for here as elsewhere black autobiography focuses on the
drama of names and naming.*

I

Like the slave narrator before him, like so many American cultural heroes, Malcolm, after the murder of his father
and the consequent psychological disintegration of his
mother and physical and psychological dissolution of his
family, the modern psychic and physical equivalent of the
slave environment, becomes an orphan who is cast into the
world alone, an innocent on his journey of initiation. Unlike
the slave narrator, who in his journey to freedom traveled
in a definite direction with the North Star as his guide,
Malcolm X's direction is less definite and is thus fraught
with attempts at finding a "home" which one by one fail
him. Initially Malcolm is totally unaware of his imprison-

ment within his social community. This unconsciousness is reflected in his innocent, unquestioning response to his earliest names, all of which symbolize his imprisonment within society's stereotypical response to him:

> At five, I, too, began to go to school, leaving home in the morning along with Wilfred, Hilda, and Philbert. It was the Pleasant Grove School that went from kindergarten through the eighth grade. It was two miles outside the city limits, and I guess there was no problem about our attending because we were the only Negroes in the area. In those days white people in the North usually would "adopt" just a few Negroes; they didn't see them as any threat. The white kids didn't make any great thing about us, either. They called us "nigger" and "darkie" and "rastus" so much we thought those were our natural names.[4]

Such lack of awareness, in part responsible for his youthful and naive thoughts of assimilation, is compounded by his lack of "color." As the lightest-skinned child in his family, Malcolm receives the unqualified affection of his father, who, the autobiographer contends,

> was subconsciously so afflicted with the white man's brainwashing of Negroes that he inclined to favor the light ones, and I was his lightest child. Most Negro parents in those days would almost instinctively treat any lighter children better than they did the darker ones. It came directly from the slavery tradition that the "mulatto," because he was visibly nearer to white, was therefore "better." (4)

Actual physical lightness only vouchsafes the possibility of "whiteness" as a viable alternative to his blackness. As the "mascot" of Mason Junior High School, Malcolm realizes that alternative to a limited extent:

> In the second semester of the seventh grade, I was elected class president. It surprised me even more than other people. But I can see now why the class might have done it. My grades were among the highest in the school. I was unique in my class, like a pink poodle. And I was proud; I'm not going to say I wasn't. In fact, by then, I didn't really have much feeling about being a Negro, because I was trying so hard, in every way I could, to be white. (31)

He plays on the basketball team, works in a restaurant, excels in school, becomes a success symbol to his own brothers and sisters and his peers. He is assimilated—as Hughes was in Harlem during the Renaissance. But, like Hughes', this "success" is deceptive and, finally, merely a chimera, for what he describes as "the first major turning point of my life" crashes down ineluctably upon him. Like so many turning points in black autobiography, young Malcolm's is a disillusioning one, stubbornly reinforcing the reality of his alienation from white society, irrevocably altering the course of his life.

An interview with his English teacher, Mr. Ostrowski, respecting his choice of a career, initiates this break:

> I know that he probably meant well in what he happened to advise me that day. I doubt that he meant any harm. It was just in his nature as an American white man. I was one of his top students, one of the school's

top students—but all he could see for me was the kind of future "in your place" that almost all white people see for black people.

He told me, "Malcolm, you ought to be thinking about a career. Have you been giving it thought?"

The truth is, I hadn't. I never have figured out why I told him. "Well, yes, sir, I've been thinking I'd like to be a lawyer." Lansing certainly had no Negro lawyers—or doctors either—in those days, to hold up an image I might have aspired to. All I really knew for certain was that a lawyer didn't wash dishes, as I was doing.

Mr. Ostrowski looked surprised, I remember, and leaned back in his chair and clasped his hands behind his head. He kind of half-smiled and said, "Malcolm, one of life's first needs is for us to be realistic. Don't misunderstand me now. We all here like you, you know that. But you've got to be realistic about being a nigger. A lawyer—that's no realistic goal for a nigger. You need to think about something you *can* be. You're good with your hands—making things. Why don't you plan on carpentry? People like you as a person—you'd get all kinds of work." (36)

The reality of "nigger" as an intractable identity in the white man's mind—no matter what external proof denies the stereotype—is borne in upon the youth. As much as he aspires to belong to white society, he never can; society only teases him into thinking it possible and then thwarts his every move to realize that dream. In fact, Malcolm's very mascotry is only another form of dehumanization, for a mascot is a thing, not an individual. Hence, this term accurately describes the naive boy's status in his social environment and becomes a synonym for "nigger," the only identity possible for him in the provincial white society, one symbolic of his real invisibility. Malcolm's early attempt at finding a place within the white community is abortive. In response, he runs to Boston, which promises to be a new, "free" home.

The slave set out for the North, Ben Franklin for Philadelphia, Booker T. Washington for Richmond, Richard Wright for Chicago, Langston Hughes for Harlem, and now Malcolm for Boston. These gifted men were not satisfied with the possibilities for growth available to them in their home towns. Each sought a more promising home environment in which to fulfill his sense of his own destiny. Malcolm, excited by the big city, soon finds that home among the inhabitants of the Roxbury ghetto: "Not only was this part of Roxbury much more exciting [than the black middle-class district] but I felt more relaxed among Negroes who were being their natural selves and not putting on airs" (43). The youth, angry and disillusioned in his attempt to gain entrance and acceptance into white society, becomes a rebel. He runs away from the assimilationist black middle-class, a surrogate of white society: he runs to the most "natural" black community. Unlike Richard Wright, whose turning point impresses upon him his alienation from any community, Malcolm finds an identity, and therefore, freedom, within this black community.

The first name Malcolm receives from his new world labels him as a "country bumpkin" uninitiated into the ways of city life: he is dubbed "Homeboy" by Shorty who becomes his first surrogate father, schooling him "to the happenings." After Homeboy's initiation into the rituals of street life, he is awarded a new name: he becomes "Red," descriptive of his bright red conked hair. But soon Boston loses its excitement, and "Red" lights out for Harlem, first as a periodical visitor while working on the trains and then as a permanent resident. Small's cafe introduces him to the regulars of the hustling trade who become his new surrogate fathers, among them Sammy the Pimp and West Indian Archie. Here, "Red" receives a new education of a very different kind: "I was thus schooled well, by experts in such hustles as the numbers, pimping, con games of many kinds, peddling dope, and thievery of all sorts, including armed robbery" (83). He is a model student who quickly becomes known and respected in the parasitical life of Harlem. As a result, "Red" gives way to "Detroit" Red to distinguish him from two other famous Red's of the ghetto, "Chicago" Red and "St. Louis" Red.

This last name can be compared and contrasted to his first one, not his given name Malcolm Little (which contains irony enough—albeit unintentional), but his first socially sanctioned name. "Nigger" designates a physical trait; as such it is a nonindividuating, collective name. In addition, it is a diminutive label, a symbol of inferiority, bestowed, at least originally, by one social group upon another rather than one social group upon itself. "Red" is also a name designating a physical trait, but, in contrast to "nigger," it is not a diminutive: it is merely a statement of physical fact, not an evaluation. "Detroit" is added to make it more selective, but, although his name is now selective rather than collective, it is still impersonal. The significant contrast is that, whereas "nigger" is an imprisoning label awarded by another society, "Detroit Red" is awarded him by his own peer group and, therefore, implies membership in and recognition by a community. Malcolm has found a new home from which he derives his sense of self-worth. The hustling life becomes the "free" life: "Every day, I cleared at least fifty or sixty dollars. . . . I felt, for the first time in my life, that great feeling of *free!*" (99). In other words, freedom derives from status in his peer group, status achieved through money (and through the companionship of white women): it is, therefore, at this point, a function of a place within the external world of the community.

II

Malcolm's rebellious flight to the freedom of the "natural" black community is, finally, a flight to criminality and, as such, is particularly significant in the context of black experience. As I have noted earlier, the ex-slave in escaping became a criminal before southern law. His criminality was the means to another way of life; it was not a way of life in itself. There was, however, a "criminal" way of life that developed within the slavocracy. The intelligent slave often became a con man, hustling his way out of work and into the "easier" life, devising ingenious ways of stealing from "old Massa" with impunity. Conning (or masking) was a form of rebellion that made the white master a party to his own deception since the mask of the "darky" symbolized the socially projected mask of the white master. The "darky" played out the master's fantasies of black identity and thereby mastered the master and gained the only self-respect available to him under the circumstances. From one point of view, as we have seen, Booker T. Washington epitomizes the ingratiating southern "darky" who conned his way to power and self-aggrandizement.

In the ghetto of the northern cities, the hustler becomes the symbol of the rebel, a black cultural hero:

Today resistance manifests itself in what whites can only see as the "social ills" of the ghetto, i.e., crime, high school dropouts, unemployment, etc. In actuality, many blacks have consciously rebelled against the system and dropped out. After all, why waste your life working at a job you hate, getting paid next to nothing, when you can make more money with half the effort. So a new class is created, the hustler who gambles, runs numbers, pushes drugs, lives off women, and does anything to avoid going to "meet the man" five days a week, year in and year out. It is a dangerous, rough, and none too beautiful life, but it has some compensation; a modicum of self-respect and the respect of a good segment of the community is gained.[5]

The hustler is a "man" who challenges rather than submits to the emasculating system; through criminality, he recovers his manhood. The young Malcolm discovers, in his role as hustler, that he need no longer be the emasculated victim but the manly victimizer, no longer the mastered but the master. The violence resulting from the confrontation of the self with a self-denying society, always threatening if not actually erupting in childhoods like that of Richard Wright, here explodes in Detroit Red's criminal existence in Harlem and Roxbury. In this role, Malcolm achieves freedom and manhood.

Criminality, however, has never been without its negative ramifications, especially when it becomes a most real aspect of daily existence, as it often does for the black American. Richard Wright in *Native Son* delineates both the positive and the negative ramifications of such criminal rebellion when it is a reality forced upon the self. Bigger may feel free when he kills; those acts of violence may be the only truly creative acts of his life. Nonetheless, he is a criminal whose criminality is literally self-destructive: he is executed by society. In fact, Bigger's violent acts are perverted acts of creation and manhood. Society has inexorably condemned him to those acts as it inexorably condemns him to death.

His violence, released in the act of murder and symbolic of the individual's confrontation with social intransigence, is essentially the violence of the victim, not of the heroic activist. For Wright, the act of criminality is both creative and self-destructive. He knows only too well from his own early experience, that criminality is a response to the destructive forces of society and that it is potentially, if not literally, self-destructive.

Similarly, the youthful Malcolm, as criminal, becomes a victim who has not, in fact, so much willed rebellion as been coerced into it. Overtly, Malcolm's hustling life seems a legitimate, liberating form of rebellion; ironically, his life as street hustler is self-destructive, conforming as it does to the norms of white society or, to put it another way, testifying as it does to an underlying belief in black inferiority. Of his first conk Malcolm explains:

> This was my first really big step toward self-degradation: when I endured all of that pain, literally burning my flesh to have it look like a white man's hair. I had joined that multitude of Negro men and women in America who are brainwashed into believing that the black people are "inferior"—and white people "superior"—that they will even violate and mutilate their God-created bodies to try to look "pretty" by white standards. (54)

The black hustler is enslaved by standards that are ordained by the white community—straight hair, money, white women. In fact, he is not free because white society determines, however obliquely, his worth.

Moreover, in attempting to outwit white society, Malcolm's own humanity is destroyed by a way of life which transforms him into a kind of animal. The autobiographer, aware of this degradation, continually describes his criminal experience in terms of animal imagery as, for example, in the following passage: "When you become an animal, a vulture, in the ghetto, as I had become, you enter a world of animals and vultures. It becomes truly the survival of the fittest" (102). Intent on survival, he becomes a predator: "I was a true hustler—uneducated, unskilled at anything honorable, and I considered myself nervy and cunning enough to live by my wits, exploiting any prey that presented itself. I would risk just about anything" (108). Such an existence becomes deadly, for he "walk[s] on [his] own coffin":

> Looking back, I think I really was at least slightly out of my mind. I viewed narcotics as most people regard food. I wore my guns as today I wear my neckties. Deep down, I actually believed that after living as fully as humanly possible, one should then die violently. I expected then, as I still expect today, to die at any time. But then, I think I deliberately invited death in many, sometimes insane ways. (138)

Spiritually and mentally dead, the victim courts physical death.

Although literal self-destruction is prevented by a prison sentence, Malcolm's spiritual depravity continues, for in prison he assumes yet another identity, that of the ultimate outlaw, Satan, who curses everyone and everything: "I would pace for hours like a caged leopard, viciously cursing aloud to myself. And my favorite targets were the Bible and God" (153). "Satan," awarded him again by his peer group, does not, as "Detroit Red" did, describe a physical characteristic; it symbolizes, instead, a spiritual state of mind, a state of mind also embodied in his description of himself as a snake. In choosing a life of crime, Malcolm has ultimately sold his soul to the devil. His physical imprisonment is the literal equivalent of his spiritual imprisonment; and, of course, the state of physical imprisonment becomes symbolic of the bars that the black American faces all his life as a second-class citizen. Prison is literal slavery; the apparently emancipated black here comes face to face with the truth of his own imprisoned self. Criminality has led not to freedom but to new forms of enslavement.

Paradoxically, literal imprisonment, first in Charleston State Prison and later in Concord Prison, becomes the condition of Malcolm X's liberation, for it is here that he comes to appreciate his real invisibility within American society and in so doing to win a viable form of freedom. Such freedom he achieves when the religious conversion to the Black Muslim faith gives new form (interpretation) to the chaos of his past. Although he does not elaborate on his spiritual conversion, he does acknowledge that "the very enormity of my previous life's guilt prepared me to accept the truth" (163), and describes the effect of the Muslim doctrine as a "blinding light." This "blinding light" radically transforms his way of seeing and the transformation in his way of seeing radically alters his identity, which, like that of the slave narrator before him, must be consecrated with a new name. For this purpose he applies for the symbolic Muslim "X," the significance of which is explained to him by his brother Reginald:

> "You don't even know who you are.... You don't even know, the white devil has hidden it from you, that you are of a race of people of ancient civilizations and riches in gold and kings. You don't even know your true family name, you wouldn't recognize your true

language if you heard it. You have been cut off by the devil white man from all true knowledge of your own kind." (161)

"Little," a name foisted upon Malcolm's ancestors by white society and as such symbolic of his continued enslavement, must be replaced by the "X," symbolic of his original though unknown African name and of his membership in the community of the "saved" (or liberated), now a totally black one.

This "X" also symbolizes Malcolm's public role as "exhorter" for this new community, a politically revolutionary one in its doctrines if not in its actions. Ironically, the motivation for his new role comes from the same source as that for his former role as criminal. Ellison alludes to the relationship between the two roles when, after the invisible man's fiery sidewalk speech in response to the eviction of the old Negro couple, Jack pursues the youth and suggests that he join the Brotherhood. Although the youth is not immediately interested, Jack persists:

> "Well, you think about it, brother. Times are grave and you seem very indignant."
> "I only wanted to make a speech," I said again.
> "But you were indignant. And sometimes the difference between individual and organized indignation is the difference between criminal and political action," he said. (223)

Malcolm X's choice of criminality, a life he found more "natural" than that of the Negro middle class, was a response, in part, of indignant anger resulting from his abortive effort to assimilate into the white society of Mason, Michigan. Ultimately, if vented in criminality, such anger is self-destructive. As, however, it is redirected into the cause of the Muslim organization, it becomes potentially con-structive.

It is no longer surprising that the Muslim doctrine should have struck Malcolm X like a "blinding light"; it gave a broader social context to his own rebellious anger, an anger overtly manifest in his speeches and covertly in his frenetic efforts at organizing. The unilateral rebellion of the crimi-nal becomes the organized ideological rebellion of a com-munity that recoils from and finally rejects its inferior status in the larger society. White society becomes a foe to be challenged, manipulated, and, finally, conquered. Conse-quently, the same skills that ensured Malcolm X's rise to prominence and success in the criminal worlds of Harlem and Boston catapult him to success and prominence in the Muslim movement. He becomes a revolutionary hustler who, instead of devoting his rational energies to his own selfish ends, sacrifices those energies to a cause. His rise to prominence, success, and leadership within the community is, therefore, quick. Malcolm X becomes a public hero, who, unlike the traditional romantic rebel in American litera-ture, sacrifices his private self to his public role in the community of rebels. This self-sacrifice is confirmed when, after his disillusioning break with Elijah Muhammad, he admits that for twelve years he had never thought for himself. In romantic rebellion, such as that of Richard Wright, self-sacrifice is self-annihilation; in revolutionary rebellion, it is self-fulfillment.

Malcolm X's autobiographical pattern recalls certain structural and thematic motifs of both the slave narrative and religious autobiography. Like the slave's escape from chattelhood to humanity, Malcolm X's escape is a spiritual one from various forms of contemporary "slavery" to a new freedom. Like the slave, he escapes one society for another which promises freedom, now reconstituted as a black militant community of the Muslim faith. His rise to prominence within that community, deriving from his public efforts in behalf of "freedom," echoes the escaped slave's rise to prominence in northern society, especially that of William Wells Brown and Frederick Douglass.

At the same time, Malcolm's experience finds parallels in the Horatio Alger autobiographical tradition, although it first turns that pattern upside down.[6] He "rises" from obscure beginnings to distinction, as Franklin and Washington before him, but that distinction, won in the criminal world of black society, is the result of cunning and conning rather than virtue and puritanical hard work. After his Muslim conversion, the pattern is reversed and a more traditional version follows, which traces his "rise" from the criminal depths of American society to prominence and acceptance within the black community. This rise is a result of his religious and political program, but his personal and public lives are patterned on Muslim mores strikingly similar to those of the Puritan and Horatio Alger hero—virtue and hard work.

> Any fornication was absolutely forbidden in the Nation of Islam. Any eating of the filthy pork, or other injurious or unhealthful foods; any use of tobacco, alcohol, or narcotics. No Muslim who followed Elijah Muhammad could dance, gamble, date, attend movies, or sports, or take long vacations from work. Muslims slept no more than health required. Any domestic quarreling, any discourtesy, especially to women, was not allowed. No lying or stealing, and no insubordination to civil authority, except on the grounds of religious obligation. (221)

Moreover, like Washington, he sees the world as material to be conquered and focuses in his autobiography, as Washington had done, on the objective facts and events of both his life of crime before conversion and his life in behalf of the Muslim organization after conversion: his operations and successes, the size of audiences, the number of cars in the caravan to Chicago, the number of temples, the growth of membership. Self-fulfillment for both men is measured in objective (public) achievements.

Resonating with this pattern is that of a sacred journey from damnation to salvation. Malcolm X's early experience culminates in a moment of enlightenment which transforms his former life into a period of sin and depravity. From that moment the "saved" autobiographer is concerned with the doctrines of his religious program: grace and salvation. Moreover, the religious self escapes the community of the damned, the worldly community (in this instance, the greater white American community), for the community of the saved or elect (the Black Muslim community). His rise to prominence after his conversion is redolent of the prominence of the elect in the Puritan community. Malcolm sacrifices himself to a public role and, in so doing, fulfills his private needs. Thus, the middle portion of the autobiography traces his arduous life as a disciple of Elijah Muhammad. Self-sacrifice becomes itself a legitimate assertion of identity.

For the most part, the journey thus far was narrated before Malcolm X's break with Elijah Muhammad became final. And, although he edited it after that break, he agreed with his assistant Alex Haley to leave his original point of view intact rather than to revise apropos of this new point of view. In the epilogue, Haley admits:

I had become worried that Malcolm X, bitter, would want to go back through the chapters in which he had told of his Black Muslim days and re-edit them in some way. The day before I left New York City to return upstate, I raised my concern to Malcolm X. "I have thought about that," he said. "There are a lot of things I could say that passed through my mind at times even then, things I saw and heard, but I threw them out of my mind. I'm going to let it stand the way I've told it. I want the book to be the way it was." (412)

What alterations he made were comments such as the one that appears at the end of the chapter entitled "Saviour" attesting to his adamantine faith in his superior. After transcribing a speech in praise of Elijah Muhammad, he continues: "This was my attitude. These were my uncompromising words, uttered anywhere, without hesitation or fear. I was his most faithful servant, and I know today that I did believe in him more firmly than he believed in himself" (210). After Malcolm's break with Elijah Muhammad does become final, however, he narrates his consequent experiences from a second, altered point of view characterized by nascent feelings of universal brotherhood that result from the second conversion, or "radical break," experienced in the very course of dictating the autobiography.

III

The slave narrator sometimes discovered that the "freedom" of northern society was only theoretical, the religious convert that his conversion had been a false one. The self could never be sure that it had achieved a truly free identity. Malcolm X, a contemporary slave narrator and a religious convert, finds, for the third time, that his freedom within the community is finally only a chimera. The community of Mason, Michigan, had been the first to reject his efforts at self-fulfillment and to send him running; the community of criminals had proved more enslaving than liberating and had finally sent him to prison; now, devastatingly, the new black community of the elect fails him. As Richard Wright had discovered at a very young age, even the black community betrays the individual's quest after authenticity. The "X" assumes ironic meanings. Originally, the quantity symbolized by the "X" was his unknown African name; later, it came to symbolize his public identity within society as an exhorter. The self-effacing hero who found authentic personal fulfillment in self-sacrifice to a public cause, now that the cause is stripped from him, is left without any sense of identity: the "X" ironically symbolizes his unknown private self. Malcolm X is an invisible man, for his identities, like those of Ellison's protagonist, have been given him by society. He does not, however, have the insight into this truth that the invisible man has.

His spiritual disillusionment is physically reflected in his breakdown, as that of Langston Hughes had been before him: "My head felt like it was bleeding inside. I felt like my brain was damaged" (303). However, the breakdown is short-lived, for Malcolm, forced once again to quest after a legitimate identity, to fill in the unknown quantity, takes to the road, running now from America to North Africa on a pilgrimage to Mecca, enacting a new version of his earlier journey from Mason, Michigan, to Boston. Once again he becomes a "Homeboy," one of the uninitiated, who is concerned, for example, with his inability to squat while saying prayers: "I never even thought about sleeping. Watched by the Muslims, I kept practicing prayer posture. I refused to let myself think how ridiculous I must have looked to them" (327). His glowing description of his reception sug-

gests his lack of sophistication and his wonderment, an echo
of his earlier wonderment at the life of the Roxbury ghetto.
And, just as his earlier journey culminated in a conversion,
so too does this second journey culminate in a radical altera-
tion:

> That morning was when I first began to reappraise the
> "white man." It was then I first began to perceive that
> "white man," as commonly used, means complexion
> only secondarily; primarily it described attitudes and
> actions. In America, "white man" meant specific at-
> titudes and actions toward the black man, and toward
> all other non-white men. But in the Muslim world, I
> had seen that men with white complexions were more
> genuinely brotherly than anyone else had ever been.
> (333-334)

With this radical break, Malcolm X feels for the first time
"like a complete human being" because for the first time he
determines his own identity, one founded not so narrowly
on race but more broadly on his humanity, and thereby he
becomes his own master: " 'I've had enough of someone
else's propaganda,' I had written to these friends. I'm for
truth, no matter who tells it. I'm for justice, no matter who it
is for or against. I'm a human being first and foremost, and
as such I'm for whoever and whatever benefits humanity *as
a whole*" (366). He is also a more complete human being
because he is no longer mastered by his anger, which is
mollified and redirected through a new experience of love
for mankind: "I was no less angry than I had been, but at
the same time the true brotherhood I had seen in the Holy
World had influenced me to recognize that anger can blind
human vision" (375).

For the fourth time, Malcolm X has escaped to a new identity, one he himself considers his truly authentic self:

> I believe that it would be almost impossible to find anywhere in America a black man who has lived further down in the mud of human society than I have; or a black man who has been any more ignorant than I have been; or a black man who has suffered more anguish during his life than I have. But it is only after the deepest darkness that the greatest joy can come; it is only after slavery and prison that the sweetest appreciation of freedom can come. (379)

And, as always, this new, "free" identity must be consummated with a name. Shedding the unknown identity "X," he adopts a name symbolizing his newfound feeling of universal brotherhood—El Hajj Malik El-Shabazz. As "Satan" in Malcolm's earlier journey had represented his spiritual nadir, so El Hajj Malik El-Shabazz represents his spiritual summit. Malcolm's autobiographical journey has led him from the socially projected, nonindividuating, and dehumanizing name of "nigger" to a name both individual and reflective of universal humanity. Moreover, his new name symbolizes an identity that is self-determined to a much greater extent than his earlier Muslim identity or any of his earlier identities, for that matter.

But even this final identity remains primarily a public one, like the earlier ones. And because his sense of personal fulfillment still emanates from a public role, Malcolm must align his somewhat private religious vision with a new public program. For this reason, he attempts to put together a new organization of the "saved." But, in spite of his attempts to found this new community, he finds himself in an essentially antinomian position, for, since he is true to his new inner light, he comes to rest outside both the black and white communities which demand certain identities of the black man, especially the black leader. With this alienation, his frustrations grow, as they must for someone dedicated to a social cause. In the epilogue, Alex Haley recalls some of this frustration:

> He talked about the pressures on him everywhere he turned, and about the frustrations, among them that no one wanted to accept anything relating to him except "my old 'hate' and 'violence' image." He said "the so-called moderate" civil-rights organizations avoided him as "too militant" and the "so-called militants" avoided him as "too moderate." "They won't let me turn the corner!" he once exclaimed, "I'm caught in a trap!" (423-424)

Malcolm X's experience, as described in the last pages of his autobiography, assumes the pattern of an antinomian struggle against society. The black leader, to fulfill the religious possibilities promised in conversion, becomes lonely and alienated from the larger community of the unsaved. Then, as a result of his efforts to recreate a responsible role within the community, he is literally sacrificed to that community. Ras the Exhorter, incarnated as Malcolm X, has been betrayed by society.

Notes

¹Ralph Ellison, *Invisible Man*, p. 177. Further citations will appear in the text.

²Ralph Ellison, "The Art of Fiction: An Interview," *Shadow and Act*, p. 177.

[3]Ibid., p. 177.

[4]Malcolm X, *The Autobiography of Malcolm X,* pp. 8-9. Further citations will appear in the text.

[5]Julius Lester, *Look Out, Whitey! Black Power's Gon' Get Your Mama,* p. 37.

[6]Carol Ohman, "The Autobiography of Malcolm X." While I do not agree with Ms. Ohman's final conclusions, I have found her article particularly useful in suggesting parallels between Malcolm X's life story and that of Washington, an autobiography also belonging to the Franklin tradition.

5

BLACK MANHOOD

"Ras recognized your black possibilities."
—*Ralph Ellison,* Invisible Man

William Wells Brown and the other escaping slaves chose to flee the South in order to recover their manhood. But when freedom proved merely chimeric, first for the escaped slave and later for the emancipated black, self-assertion continued to be potentially self-destructive. Consequently, the price of sheer survival over the years had been and continued to be emasculation of the black man. Malcolm X's legacy was this very manhood: his autobiographical experience attests to the black man's infrangible spirit, to his ability to free himself from imprisonment and to recreate himself again and again, if need be, in continual acts of renewal and rebirth until he is reborn, finally, into full black manhood. Ossie Davis writes of Malcolm X that "whatever else he was or was not—Malcolm was a man." He continues:

White folks do not need anybody to remind them that they are men. We do! This was his one incontrovertible benefit to his people.

Protocol and common sense require that Negroes stand back and let the white man speak up for us, defend us, and lead us

*from behind the scene in our fight. This is the essence of Negro
politics. But Malcolm said to hell with that! Get up off your
knees and fight your own battles. That's the way to win back
your self-respect.* [1]

*Racial pride is the primary manifestation of such self-respect,
self-hatred the primary manifestation of historical emasculation. As
Ras the Exhorter says to Tod Clifton whom he meets during a street
fight between the nationalists and the Brotherhood,*

> *"You young and intelligent. You black and beautiful—don't
> let 'em tell you different! You wasn't them t'ings you be dead,
> mahn. Dead! I'd have killed you, mahn. . . . Ras recognized
> your black possibilities, mahn. Ras would not sacrifice his
> black brother to the white enslaver. Instead he* cry. *Ras is a
> mahn—no white mahn have to tell him that—and Ras* cry. *So
> why don't you recognize your black duty, and come jine us?"*
> *(282)*

*The black American achieves real freedom in the process of recover-
ing his manhood. And as Ras the Exhorter makes clear, this process
is linked inevitably with the recovery of racial pride. The very
process is the underlying organic pattern of Eldridge Cleaver's
autobiography,* Soul On Ice.

I

Characteristically, Cleaver's spiritual escape to freedom
originates in a physical confinement that forces him to confront the hard reality of his spiritual confinement within
American society; since Cleaver's road to freedom is indeter-
minate, his journey, like that of Malcolm X, is not without
its abortive attempts. The first of these he describes in the
opening letter in which he returns to 1954, the symbolic

and historic beginning of his spiritual journey. That year marked a turning point in Afro-American history and a turning point in Cleaver's own personal history, for in 1954, when the controversial Supreme Court decision on segregation is made, the eighteen-year-old Cleaver is imprisoned for possession of drugs. While witnessing the controversy over the court decision from behind bars, Cleaver comes to realize that, prior to 1954, he in particular and black Americans in general had "lived in an atmosphere of novocain," anesthetized by the historical necessity of maintaining some kind of sanity in the face of social brutalization, by the necessity of survival itself. The court decision forces Cleaver's consciousness out from under this anesthesia: "This controversy awakened me to my position in America and I began to form a concept of what it meant to be black in white America."[2] As he comes to realize that, after almost one hundred years of freedom, the black American is still enslaved in his socially projected identity, he comes to understand that his identity, his destiny, is linked inextricably with whatever identity and destiny is achieved by his race. Overwhelmed by such knowledge and its upshot, a scathing anger, Cleaver willfully rebels against society by "turn[ing] away from America with horror, or disgust and outrage" (4). Moreover, he chooses to rebel, as the slave before him, alone: "I decided the only safe thing for me to do was to go for myself" (5). For Cleaver, the rebel's definitive expression of freedom is individual, "unilateral" *action* as opposed to *reaction,* for action guarantees the freedom of self-determination whereas reaction involves an admission of coercive imprisonment.

But first, the angered rebel learns just how imprisoned he is: "In prison, those things withheld from and denied to the prisoner become precisely what he wants most of all, of course" (6). Having chosen a pinup of a white girl to hang in his cell, he is shocked into a devastating self-consciousness when the prison guard demands that he find a black one, for he must admit to himself that he actually prefers white women. His reaction to the white woman, whom he re-names "The Ogre," symbolizes the slave's response to the dominant society. Here, the literal prison becomes a strik-ing metaphor for American society in general, which has "indoctrinated [him] to see the white woman as more beau-tiful and desirable than [his] own black woman" (10). Later, as he reads the newspaper account of the murder in Missis-sippi of Emmett Till, a black youth from Chicago, and then looks at the photograph of the white woman with whom Till had "allegedly" flirted, Cleaver is overcome by his emo-tional response:

> I felt that little tension in the center of my chest I experience when a woman appeals to me. I was dis-gusted and angry with myself. Here was a woman who had caused the death of a black, possibly because when he looked at her, he also felt the same tensions of lust and desire in his chest—and probably for the same general reasons that I felt them. It was all unacceptable to me. I looked at the picture again and again, and in spite of everything and against my will and the hate I felt for the woman and all that she represented, she appealed to me. I flew into a rage at myself, at America, at white women, at the history that had placed those tensions of lust and desire in my chest. (11)

His rage at such psychological slavery precipitates a nervous breakdown, a characteristic moment in black au-tobiography, which in turn precipitates a radical revision of his thought, a revision further stimulated when, after his discharge from the prison hospital, he resumes his readings and eventually finds verification for his contempt and hatred of American society in the critical analysis of capitalism delineated in certain books. As a result, he becomes a revolutionary socialist, who, like the slave narrator, rebels against society, but, unlike the slave narrator, does not seek the community of another society. Instead, he fashions an identity around the concept of the outlaw, one previously analyzed in connection with Malcolm X:

> Somehow I arrived at the conclusion that, as a matter of principle, it was of paramount importance for me to have an antagonistic, ruthless attitude toward white women. The term *outlaw* appealed to me and at the time my parole date was drawing near, I considered myself to be mentally free—I was an "outlaw." I had stepped outside of the white man's law, which I repudiated with scorn and self-satisfaction. I became a law unto myself—my own legislature, my own supreme court, my own executive. (13)

Significantly, Cleaver links rebellion against American society, or rather American capitalism, with a "ruthless attitude toward white women." For Cleaver, slavery to the white woman symbolizes his enslavement to capitalism: politics and sexual relationships become the two sides of the same coin. Hence, upon his release from prison, he deliberately chooses rape as a revolutionary act that embodies his new sense of liberation from the American system. Whereas Malcolm X's criminality had been an unconscious response to his abortive attempt to assimilate into white society, Cleaver's is not unconscious; it is willed rebellion:

> It delighted me that I was defying and trampling upon

the white man's law, upon his system of values, and that I was defiling his women—and this point, I believe, was the most satisfying to me because I was very resentful over the historical fact of how the white man has used the black woman. I felt I was getting revenge. From the site of the act of rape, consternation spreads outwardly in concentric circles. I wanted to send waves of consternation throughout the white race. (14)

In fact, Cleaver's "revolutionary" act of rape is reactionary. Like Malcolm X's criminality, it is not real but rather false freedom, another, more self-destructive form of oppression which catapults him back to literal imprisonment. The way to freedom is not reactionary escape but direct confrontation with a self and a society that are sick.

His own sickness has two manifestations relevant to the thematic and structural organization of his autobiography, both of them symbolized in the act of rape itself. First, the rape of a white woman by a black man is a form of communication; but the impulse that motivates such communication is certainly not love. Cleaver describes this impulse as "bloody, hateful, bitter and malignant," and concludes that "whites would really be hard pressed to find it flattering" (17). Secondly, rape is a sexual crime that betrays a perverted sense of masculinity, an animality that corroborates the myth surrounding black sexuality. As a rapist, Cleaver merely perpetuates and reinforces the myth.

These two factors combine to provide the initial portrait of Cleaver as a hate-ridden animal, a portrait precisely like that which Malcolm X draws of himself in his criminality. Cleaver characterizes this early life before conversion as the life of depravity—of evil, hatred, and animal lust—and confesses that he "also learned that it is easier to do evil than it is to do good" (15). The most demoralizing result of this sickness is that he becomes less than human by going astray of his humanity and, in so doing, forfeits his self-respect and pride: "The price of hating other human beings is loving oneself less" (17). Moreover, in becoming less than a man, he has, ironically, reaffirmed the accuracy of white society's myths. Again, he is stripped of his own self-respect: "My pride as a man dissolved and my whole fragile moral structure seemed to collapse, completely shattered" (15).

This second breakdown, a physical manifestation of a radical break with his former identity, initiates a quest for a new, more authentic one, a quest focused, as in the slave narrative, on the discovery of a primary identity. Thus, he envisions his search as one to answer that persistent question, "What am I?": "I had to find out who I am and what I want to be, what type of man I should be, and what I could do to become the best of which I am capable" (15). This search is linked here, as elsewhere in black autobiography, with the theme of naming when he says of himself: "I was very familiar with the Eldridge who came to prison, but that Eldridge no longer exists. And the one I am now is in some ways a stranger to me" (16). He must discover the self his name defines. This process of redefinition he associates with another name, "Lazarus," which becomes an appropriate metaphor for the black man who, having been dead to his full manhood for hundreds of years, is being resurrected. Initially, Cleaver himself is the dead Lazarus, separated as he is from a feeling of wholeness:

> I was twenty-two when I came to prison and of course I have changed tremendously over the years. But I had always had a strong sense of myself and in the last few years I felt that I was losing my identity. There was a deadness in my body that eluded me, as though I could

not exactly locate its site. I would be aware of this numbness, this feeling of atrophy, and it haunted the back of my mind. Because of this numb spot, I felt peculiarly off balance, the awareness of something missing, of a blank spot, a certain intimation of emptiness. (24-25)

He must resurrect the dead part of himself to be the reborn Lazarus, the new "Eldridge."

His central spiritual concern, therefore, will be to resurrect himself; he can do so only by regaining his black manhood, an act that involves healing the breach between his body and his mind created by slavery and perpetuated by capitalism and substituting the communication of love for the communication of hate. Imprisoned in his hatred and his animality, in his own "South," Cleaver must discover an escape route to the freedom of the "North." Because he cannot escape physically, he must find the escape through self-analysis and social analysis. For Cleaver, the quest for identity is the corollary of the understanding of social and political history; and so, just as the religious convert discovers his true self in his religious role, so does Cleaver discover his free self through his social vision.

II

In the title letter, "Soul On Ice," Cleaver eloquently confesses love for his lawyer, an intimation that he has indeed begun the process of rebirth. He responds to her intellectually, seeing in her alienated relationship to society an echo of his own, but recognizing that she turns such alienation to more positive ends:

My lawyer is not an ordinary person. My lawyer is a

rebel, a revolutionary who is alienated fundamentally
from the status quo, probably with as great an intensity,
conviction, and irretrievability as I am alienated from
it—and probably with more intelligence, compassion,
and humanity. (21)

Cleaver himself has been an irresponsible rebel, motivated
only by hate; Beverly Axelrod, on the other hand, rebels
responsibly with humanity and intelligence. Furthermore,
his response to her is emotional as well. Thus, the fact that
she is white makes the involvement potentially rejuvenat-
ing, for in truly caring for the very type of person who has
previously been the victim of his inhumanity, he may regain
that humanity and self-respect. She is not "The Ogre"; she
is "Beverly Axelrod," a separate individual whom he regards as a person rather than as a white. She, too, regards
him as a man rather than as a black. He is, so to speak,
brought back to life by this woman who becomes a modern
Madonna, or Beatrice, leading him out from the limbo of
hatred into the light of love, a salvational role suggested by
his own language:

> Yet I may believe that a man whose soul or emotional
> apparatus had lain dormant in a deadening limbo of
> desuetude is capable of responding from some great
> sunken will of his being, as though a potent catalyst had
> been tossed into a critical mass, when an exciting,
> lovely, and lovable woman enters the range of his feel-
> ings. What a deep, slow, torturous, reluctant, fright-
> ened stirring! He feels a certain part of himself in a
> state of flux, as if a bodiless stranger has stolen inside
> his body, startling him by doing calisthenics, and he
> feels himself coming slowly back to life. His body

chemistry changes and he is flushed with new strength.
(23)

Lazarus commences his journey back from the dead.

In actuality, this letter is dated several months later than the subsequent letters in part I. It functions here to foreshadow his final recovery from the hate-ridden stance of the black nationalist and black racist, a public and private identity Cleaver accepts while in prison. As a convert to the Black Muslim religion, he finds self-definition through his rigid, confining racial identity. Whereas his first form of rebellion had taken him outside the entire American community, his second rebellious identity alienates him completely from American society in general but puts him solidly inside a much more limited community of Black Muslim converts who have seen the "light" of Elijah Muhammad. The letters following the title piece recall particularly meaningful moments in his experience as a Muslim, culminating in the letter, "The Christ and His Teachings," which reveals his stance as a disciple of war engaged in open warfare with all white people: "All the gods were dead except the god of war" (34). In response to an assignment by his teacher (whom the inmates nickname "The Christ"), Cleaver writes an essay in which he states unequivocally that he cannot love white people, that he can, in fact, only hate them.

This peremptory hatred is eventually reassessed in lieu of the schism between Elijah Muhammad and Malcolm X. Cleaver chooses to support Malcolm X, thus finding release from a consuming black racism. He realizes that "there were those of us who were glad to be liberated from a doctrine of hate and racial supremacy. The onus of teaching racial supremacy and hate, which is the white man's burden, is pretty hard to bear" (57). However, the redefinition necessary after such a liberation is not immediately forthcoming. As he says himself: "Having renounced the teachings of Elijah Muhammad, I find that a rebirth does not follow automatically, of its own accord, that a void is left in one's vision, and this void seeks constantly to obliterate itself by pulling one back to one's former outlook" (66). Again the black self is forced to recreate itself anew after a radical break. Cleaver had tried to define himself, as did Malcolm X, in terms of his public identity as a Black Muslim, in this way fashioning an identity out of a socio-religious cause. And, like that of Malcolm X after his break with Elijah Muhammad, Cleaver's identity, which he equates with his "vision," vanishes when the allegiance to the cause vanishes: the self becomes a void.

The new "Eldridge" emerges as a socialist critic and revolutionary prophet; his vision, the substance of his essays, becomes his new identity because, in understanding the world by means of that vision, he comes to understand himself. As a socialist critic, Cleaver is a contemporary slave narrator whose purpose, like that of his predecessors, is to expose the truth that America's sickness is a direct outgrowth of the system of capitalism at home and imperialism abroad, which perpetuates the master-slave syndrome and, like slavery, views men as materials to be owned and exploited. The legacy of such a system is the emasculation of the "slave," in this instance, the black man. The "slave's" manhood must, therefore, be resurrected, no matter what the cost. Such rebirth can be effected only by the reunification of the mind and the body; for according to Cleaver's analysis, the white man has maintained omnipotence in American society by usurping the "mind" and delegating the "body" (brute force) to the black man, the vestige of a slave system which considered the black man merely a beast of burden. America's sickness is, in effect, the sickness that separates the two halves of a whole being, that views the mind as superior to the body, the body, as something to be denied, suppressed. The black man, relegated to brute status, is first of all castrated from his intellect, and second of all, suspect in a society that shuns sexuality. Two myths perpetuate this sickness and thwart black attempts at reunification: the myth of Negro sexuality condemns the black man to perpetual physicality; the myth of inferiority disassociates him from half of himself, his mind. The black man and woman are therefore profoundly alienated from half of themselves and castigated for the half from which they are not alienated. The myths, projective fantasies of white men, make a lie of democracy and equality, and that lie makes American society schizophrenic.

Self-hatred and its corollary, escape from blackness, is the most destructive result of the black man's continued emasculation. Cleaver elaborates on this theme in "Notes of a Native Son," an essay in which he characterizes James Baldwin as an intellectual Tom:

> The racial death-wish is manifested as the driving force in James Baldwin. His hatred for blacks, even as he pleads what he conceives as their cause, makes him the apotheosis of the dilemma in the ethos of the black bourgeoisie who have completely rejected their African heritage, consider the loss irrevocable, and refuse to look again in that direction. (103)

He contends that what Baldwin hates in Richard Wright is Wright's masculinity; obviously, what Cleaver hates in Baldwin is his homosexuality, a failure of masculinity that he equates with self-hate and, in the black man, with black-hate.

The resurrection of potency, masculinity, and self-worth is the theme of "Lazarus, Come Forth," which focuses on the boxing match as the ultimate test of masculinity in American society. Here the black American is allowed to excel, for the boxing ring is an apolitical arena. In the political arena, however, black self-assertion is destroyed by social ostracism, expatriation, assassination. In this context the Clay-Patterson fight becomes highly significant, for Clay represents the autonomous black man who is political, who is not, like Patterson, controlled by an (invisible) white man, who has a mind of his own by which to outwit his opponent, and who, therefore, has power over himself. Clay is his own master, another resurrected Lazarus, who, in changing his name to Muhammad Ali, rejects his former, dead identity and adopts a new one appropriate to his rebirth. Moreover, this resurrection in America finds parallels in the international scene. As a socialist critic Cleaver does not limit himself to the national scene, for the national movement and the international movements of liberation are linked. They are movements against capitalism and its bedfellow imperialism, against the system that emasculates men and keeps them in psychological, if not in literal, chains.

"Prelude to Love" goes on to suggest that true communication between black and white is possible. Beverly Axelrod responds to Cleaver as a whole man: "Your manhood comes through in a thousand ways, rare and wonderful" (145). Cleaver's response to her is one of love, a sharp contrast to his earlier response of rape. This transcendence is a sign of health—his own and perhaps, ultimately, that of the world:

We represent historical forces and it is really these forces that are coalescing and moving toward each

other. And it is not a fraud, forced out of desperation.
We live in a disoriented, deranged social structure, and
we have transcended its barriers in our own ways and
have stepped psychologically outside its madness and
repressions. (150)

Axelrod is the white woman responding to the black man's
whole manhood, intellectual as well as physical: he is the
black man responding to the white woman, spiritually as
well as physically. Through their relationship, the oppressive social myths have been transcended; black and white
join in a constructive rather than a destructive union.

After this lyric interlude, symbolic of Cleaver's convalescence, he can in part IV reconsider "The Ogre" in a confrontation with the sexual sickness of American society.
"The Allegory of the Black Eunuchs" is an imaginative
fiction in which three youths confront the disturbing presence of a castrated, aged black man, the Lazarus who has
survived in a castrating system because he has remained
"dead." They are confronted, furthermore, with the de-
tailed reality of the black man's love for the white woman:

> "I'd jump over ten nigger bitches just to get to one
> white woman. Ain't no such thing as an ugly white
> woman. A white woman is beautiful even if she's bald-
> headed and only has one tooth. . . . It's not just the fact
> that she's a woman that I love; I love her skin, her soft,
> smooth, white skin. I like to just lick her white skin as if
> sweet, fresh honey flows from her pores, and just to
> touch her long, soft, silky hair. There's a softness about
> a white woman, something delicate and soft inside her.
> But a nigger bitch seems to be full of steel, granite-hard
> and resisting, not soft and submissive like a white
> woman. Ain't nothing more beautiful than a white

woman's hair being blown by the wind. The white woman is more than a woman to me. . . . She's like a goddess, a symbol. My love for her is religious and beyond fulfillment. I worship her. I love a white woman's dirty drawers." (159)

Fear of a similar response is expressed by the young "blood" narrating the tale:

Then the Infidel looked up and locked my eyes with his own. A cruel, wounded expression was in his eyes. I could see a pain there that was dreadful. It made me feel fear—not so much for the Infidel as for myself, my generation, my contemporaries, because I was not sure that I, we, knew what to do or would learn before it was too late, and would be able to escape from feeling that same deep-seated pain some day, myself, ourselves. (166)

The Infidel disgusts the youths precisely because he is a mirror in which they can see their potential selves. In reaction, they reject him cruelly, calling for the blood of the slavemaster in order to avoid such emasculation. This is Cleaver's imaginative recapitulation of his own experience.

In "The Primeval Mitosis," Cleaver elaborates more fully the four-way sexual-racial relationship introduced by the old man in the previous essay. As he has explained earlier, American society is sick because of the unnatural split that has occurred between the mind and body, the former appropriated by the white man in power, the latter delegated to the black beast of burden. Such an unnatural split alienates one half of the self from its other half: the white man from his body, the black man from his mind. Now, however, Cleaver shifts his strategy from attacking whites because they have denied blacks a mind to attacking them because they have no sense of a body. He suggests that the black man and woman are more "natural' than the "de-essenced" white man; this vitality, suspect before in society, becomes its salvation. Cleaver echoes earlier black writers such as Countee Cullen and especially Jean Toomer whose *Cane*, written during the Harlem Renaissance of the 1920s, embodies a schema which associates positive values, such as brotherhood and creativity, with passionate, virile black society and negative values with sterile, conventional industrialized white society. In "Convalescence," Cleaver sees the remedy for American society in this very vitality. He returns again to the 1954 Supreme Court decision that introduces his autobiography and which now comes to symbolize a surgical operation meant "to graft the nation's Mind back unto its Body and vice versa" (192). As an example of this revitalization, Cleaver humorously describes the phenomenon of the Twist, the dance through which the white was made to feel his body once again. The hip-swinging freedom of movement of the dance becomes an electrifying healer of America's ailment, the sterile frigidity of rigidly structured white society alienated from its deepest impulses.

Since 1954 Cleaver has been operating on himself —reuniting his mind and body and thus gaining the freedom of wholeness. What he says of the Supermasculine Menial in "The Primeval Mitosis" is autobiographical: "The struggle of his life is for the emancipation of his mind, and official recognition of the fact that he has a mind" (186). The essays dramatize this very emancipation of mind—in a context in which the body continues to be recognized and celebrated. A new "Eldridge," his mind released from "Cold Storage," has "returned from the dead" and can now stand before the black woman proudly, can write the last letter, "To All Black Women, From All Black Men":

> I greet you, my Queen, not in the obsequious whine of
> a cringing Slave to which you have become accus-
> tomed, neither do I greet you in the new voice, the
> unctuous supplications of the sleek Black Bourgeoisie,
> nor the bullying bellow of the rude Free Slave—but in
> my own voice do I greet you, the voice of the Black
> Man. And although I greet you anew, my greeting is
> not new, but as old as the Sun, Moon, and Stars. And
> rather than mark a new beginning, my greeting sig-
> nifies only my Return. (205)

Finally, "Eldridge" is free of The Ogre whose appeal has
symbolized a self-hating flight from blackness toward
whiteness. No longer does he yearn to escape his racial
identity, for, through a new myth, blackness becomes
superior to whiteness because it is more natural, more
genuinely whole or "one." Cleaver has become the Prince,
the new mythical hero to whom Ras the Exhorter appeals.
In this public role, he achieves real freedom. He remains
outside American society, now by choice rather than by
coercion, where he seeks to establish a new revolutionary
community of resurrected selves, one, unlike the Black
Muslim community, open to all who liberate themselves
from the master-slave syndrome.

III

The black self rebels with its mind and, in so doing,
recovers manhood, a manhood predicated on the reunification of the mind and body. Through his public role as
revolutionary social critic, Cleaver finally feels his full mas-

culinity, the masculinity of the black man as black leader, no longer emasculated, no longer afraid to unmask the true nature and extent of his rebellion. Cleaver's original expression of revolutionary action led him to choose the public role of rapist, which only reinforced the stereotype of black sexuality and, simultaneously, diminished his humanity: he communicated with white society in a violently physical and ultimately self-destructive and counterproductive way. Now, in analyzing American society and communicating with it through writing, he uses his intellect rather than his body and, as a result, discovers an infinitely more self-fulfilling and productive form of rebellion. Cleaver's anger, like Wright's and Malcolm X's before him, finally channels itself into the word, a much more effective weapon through which to make his public statement (assault), both his prophesies of hope and his more scathing prophesies of doom. Moreover, the very act of writing confounds the stereotype of black inferiority by attesting to Cleaver's intellectuality. Therefore it is a political act. Because writing evidences intellect in a society that refuses to acknowledge the intellect of the black, it becomes a radical form of rebellion, one that calls to mind a primary political motivation of the slave narrator. As Douglass makes explicit, the slave narrative was an effective weapon that testified to the ex-slave's educability and intellectual capacities.

In a certain sense, Cleaver's is no conventional autobiography. He offers no facts about his background, family, youth and so on. But *Soul On Ice* joins such recent autobiographical writings as George Jackson's *Soledad Brother* and LeRoi Jones' *Home* among others, writings that are not so much histories of individuals as they are social analyses of American racism. And yet, this tradition in black American autobiographical writing is really at the center of its impulse. In society where blackness is met with implicit and explicit forms of racism, the understanding of that very racism, its motivations, its effects upon the self and the society at large, is tantamount to the understanding of one's identity. In the process of imposing the order of an analysis upon the complex manifestations of American racism, Cleaver and other black Americans impose order on the chaos engulfing them and, as a result, come to understand themselves; they know who they are and why they are who they are. In fact, this tradition goes back to the slave narratives. Frederick Douglass, as did many other slave narrators, makes his own acute analysis of the effects of slavery upon both the white and black communities. W.E.B. DuBois in writing his autobiography, *Dusk of Dawn*, subtitled it *An Essay Toward the Autobiography of a Race Concept* and eschewed his own personal life to discuss the experiences that formed the intellectual construct through which he came to view his environment. Cleaver gives us a more contemporary version of this impulse in black autobiography.

Notes

[1]Ossie Davis, "On Malcolm X," in *The Autobiography of Malcolm X*, pp. 457-458.
[2]Eldridge Cleaver, *Soul On Ice*, p. 3. Further citations will appear in the text.

6

BLACK
WOMANHOOD

But put on your crown, my queen.
                    —Eldridge Cleaver, Soul On Ice

Eldridge Cleaver concludes his spiritual journey when he is prepared to greet the black queen in the voice of the new "Eldridge," the black man who is secure in both his physical and intellectual masculinity. But the black woman has also to make her own spiritual journey, for the Amazon, as Cleaver labels her,

is in a peculiar position. Just as her man has been deprived of his manhood, so she has been deprived of her full womanhood. Society has decreed that the Ultrafeminine, the woman of the elite, is the goddess on the pedestal. The Amazon is the personification of the rejected domestic component, the woman on whom "dishpan hands" seems not out of character. The worship and respect which both the Omnipotent Administrator and the Supermasculine Menial lavish upon the image of the Ultrafeminine is a source of deep vexation to the Amazon. She envies the pampered, powder-puff existence of the Ultrafeminine and longs to incorporate these elements into her own life. Alienated from the feminine component of her na-

121

*ture, her reinforced domestic component is an awesome burden
and shame of which she longs to be free. (188)*

*The oppression of natural forces, of physical appearance and
processes, foists a self-consciousness on all young girls who must
grow from children into women. But in the black girl child's
experience these natural forces are reinforced by the social forces of
racial subordination and impotence. Being born black is itself a
liability in a world ruled by white standards of beauty which
imprison the black girl in a cage of ugliness at birth. "Caught in the
crossfire of masculine prejudice, white illogical hate, and Black
lack of power," the black and blue bruises of her soul multiply and
compound as she flings herself against the bars of her cage.*[1]

I

Maya Angelou's autobiography, *I Know Why the Caged
Bird Sings,* like Wright's *Black Boy,* opens with a primal
childhood scene that brings into focus the nature of the
imprisoning environment from which the black girl child
seeks to escape. The young, awkward Maya, dressed in a
cut-down, faded purple, too-long taffeta gown, stands
nervously before an Easter congregation in Stamps, Arkansas, reciting a poem, asking "What you looking at me for?"
She cannot remember the next lines, and so this question
imprints itself indelibly on the shame-filled silence. Finally,
the minister's wife offers her the forgotten lines. She grabs
them, spills them into the congregation and then stumbles
out of the watching church, "a green persimmon caught
between [her] legs." Unable to control the pressure of her
physical response, she urinates, then laughs "from the
knowledge that [she] wouldn't die from a busted head."
But the cathartic laughter never even begins to mute,

much less transcend, the real pain that is this experience, the palpable pain that pulses through her long trip down the aisle of that singing church as urine flows down her grotesquely skinny, heavily dusted legs. "What you looking at *me* for?"—over and over until it becomes, "Is something *wrong* with me?" For this child, too much is wrong.

The whole way she looks is wrong, and she knows it. That is why they are all looking at her. Earlier, as she watches her grandmother make over the white woman's faded dress, she revels for one infinitely delicious moment in fantasies of stardom. In a beautiful dress, she would be transformed into a beautiful movie star: "I was going to look like one of the sweet little white girls who were everybody's dream of what was right with the world" (4). But between the taffeta insubstantiality of her ideal vision of herself and the raw (fleshy) edges of her substantiality stands the one-way mirror:

> Easter's early morning sun had shown the dress to be a plain ugly cut-down from a white woman's once-was-purple throwaway. It was old-lady-long too, but it didn't hide my skinny legs, which had been greased with Blue Seal Vaseline and powdered with the Arkansas red clay. The age-faded color made my skin look dirty like mud, and everyone in church was looking at my skinny legs. (4)

Wrong dress. Wrong legs. Wrong hair. Wrong face. Wrong color. The child lives a "black ugly dream," a nightmare. But since this life is only a dream, the child knows she will awaken soon into a rightened, a whitened reality:

> Wouldn't they be surprised when one day I woke out of my black ugly dream, and my real hair, which was long

and blond, would take the place of the kinky mass that
Momma wouldn't let me straighten? My light-blue eyes
were going to hypnotize them, after all the things they
said about "my daddy must of been a Chinaman" (I
thought they meant made out of china, like a cup)
because my eyes were so small and squinty. Then they
would understand why I had never picked up a Southern accent, or spoke the common slang, and why I had
to be forced to eat pigs' tails and snouts. Because I was
really white and because a cruel fairy stepmother, who
was understandably jealous of my beauty, had turned
me into a too-big Negro girl, with nappy black hair,
broad feet and a space between her teeth that would
hold a number two pencil. (4-5)

In a society attuned to white standards of physical beauty,
the black girl child cries herself to sleep at night to the tune
of her own inadequacy. At least she can gain temporary
respite in the impossible dreams of whiteness. Here in the
darkened nights of the imagination, that refuge from society and the mirror, blossoms an ideal self. Yet even the
imagination is sometimes not so much a refuge as it is a
prison in which the dreamer becomes even more inescapa-
bly possessed by the nightmare, since the very self he fan-
tasizes conforms perfectly to society's prerequisites. The
cage door jangles shut around the child's question: "What
you looking at me for?"

This opening to Maya Angelou's autobiography recreates vividly the dynamics of the black girl child's imprisonment in American society. Grier and Cobbs summarize
this predicament of the black woman in *Black Rage*:

If the society says that to be attractive is to be white, she
finds herself unwittingly striving to be something she

cannot possibly be; and if femininity is rooted in feeling oneself eminently lovable, then a society which views her as unattractive and repellent has also denied her this fundamental wellspring of femininity.[2]

Maya is a black ugly reality, not a whitened dream. And the attendant self-consciousness and diminished self-image throb through her bodily prison until the bladder can do nothing but explode in a parody of release. Such momentary freedom from the physical pressure of her displacement becomes a kind of metaphor for the freedom from the psychological pressure of her displacement after which she will quest.

II

After establishing the psychic environment out of which the black girl child must achieve maturity, against which she must struggle for selfhood, Angelou returns to the beginning of her quest. Two children, sent away to a strange place by estranging parents, cling to each other as they travel by train across the southwestern United States—and cling to their tag: " 'To Whom It May Concern'—that we were Marguerite and Bailey Johnson, Jr., from Long Beach, California, en route to Stamps, Arkansas, c/o Mrs. Annie Henderson" (6). The autobiography of black America is haunted by these orphans, descendants of the orphaned slave narrators, who travel through life desperately in search of a home where they can escape the shadow of lonely displacement. Although Maya and Bailey are traveling toward the home of their grandmother, it is more significant that they are traveling away from the home of their parents. A child may internalize and translate such rejection into rejection of self; thus, the loss of home ultimately occasions the loss of self-worth. For this reason, the quest for a new home is tantamount to the quest for acceptance, for love, and for the resultant feeling of self-worth. Like that of any orphan's, such a quest is intensely solitary, making it all the more desperate, immediate, and demanding, and, making it, above all, an even more estranging process. So long as the "place" is conceived as a function of others' (society's) acceptance, it always recedes into the distance, moving with the horizon, as the "North" receded for the escaped slave and later for the free black American.

Stamps, Arkansas, does not offer a sense of place to Maya:

> The town reacted to us as its inhabitants had reacted to all things new before our coming. It regarded us a while without curiosity but with caution, and after we were seen to be harmless (and children) it closed in around us, as a real mother embraces a stranger's child. Warmly, but not too familiarly. (7)

The aura of personal displacement is counterpointed by the ambience of displacement within the larger black community of Stamps, which is itself caged in the social reality of racial subordination and impotence. The cotton pickers must face an empty bag every morning, an empty will every night, knowing all along that they would end the season as they had begun it—with no money and no credit. This undercurrent of social displacement, this fragility of the sense of belonging, are evidenced in the intrusion of white reality. Poor white trash humiliate Momma as she stands erect before them singing a hymn. Uncle Willie hides deep in the potato barrel the night the sheriff warns them that white men ride after black, any black. The white apparition haunts the life of Stamps, Arkansas, always present though not always visible.

Against this apparition, the community shores itself up with a subdued hominess, a fundamental faith in a fundamental religion, and resignation. The warmth mitigates the need to resist, or, rather, the impossibility of resistance is sublimated in the bond of community. The people of Stamps, including Momma Henderson, adapt in the best way they know—"realistically": Momma "didn't cotton to the idea that white-folks could be talked to at all without risking one's life. And certainly they couldn't be spoken to insolently" (46). If the young girl stands before the church congregation asking, "What you looking at me for?" the whole black community might just as well be standing before the larger white community and asking that same question. High physical visibility means self-consciousness within the white community. To insure his own survival, the black tries not to be looked at, tries to become invisible. Such a necessary response breeds an overriding self-criticism and self-depreciation into the black experience. Maya Angelou's diminished self-image reflects at the same time that it is reinforced by the entire black community's diminished self-image.

Nevertheless, there is a containedness in this environment called Stamps, just as there was in the black community surrounding young Richard Wright, a containedness which in this case mitigates rather than intensifies the child's sense of displacement. Here is a safe way of life, certainly a hard way of life, but finally a known way of life. Maya, like Richard, does not really want to fit here, but the town shapes her to it. And although she is lonely and suffers from her feelings of ugliness and abandonment, the strength of Momma's arms contains some of that loneliness.

Then suddenly Stamps is left behind as Maya moves to another promise of place, to her mother, aunts, uncles, grandparents, and St. Louis. But even here there is displacement since St. Louis remains a foreign country to the child, with its strange sounds, its packaged foods, its modern conveniences:

> In my mind I only stayed in St. Louis for a few weeks. As quickly as I understood that I had not reached my home, I sneaked away to Robin Hood's forest and the caves of Alley Oop where all reality was unreal and even that changed every day. I carried the same shield that I had used in Stamps: "I didn't come to stay." (68)

For one moment only, the illusion of being in place overwhelms the child. For that moment Mr. Freeman, her mother's boyfriend, holds her pressed to him:

> He held me so softly that I wished he wouldn't ever let me go. I felt at home. From the way he was holding me I knew he'd never let me go or let anything bad ever happen to me. This was probably my real father and we had found each other at last. But then he rolled over, leaving me in a wet place and stood up. (71)

The orphan hopes, for that infinite moment, that she has been taken back home to her father; she feels loved, wanted, special, lovely. Ultimately Mr. Freeman's arms are not succor, but seduction: the second time he holds Maya to him it is to rape her. In short minutes, Maya becomes even more displaced: she becomes a child-woman. Moreover, she is doubly victimized by the experience. As a female child, she is subject to the physical superiority of the male. Then later, when she denies the first incident in court and

Mr. Freeman is afterwards found dead, she connects his death with her lie and is psychologically victimized. Her only recourse is to stop talking: "Just my breath, carrying my words out, might poison people and they'd curl up and die like the black fat slugs that only pretended. I had to stop talking" (85).

In total solitude, total self-condemnation, total silence, Maya retreats to Stamps, to gray barren nothingness:

> The resignation of its inhabitants encouraged me to relax. They showed me a contentment based on the belief that nothing more was coming to them, although a great deal more was due. Their decision to be satisfied with life's inequities was a lesson for me. Entering Stamps, I had the feeling that I was stepping over the border lines of the map and would fall, without fear, right off the end of the world. Nothing more could happen, for in Stamps nothing happened. (86)

Her psychological and emotional devastation find a mirror in Stamps' social devastation. Stamps returns Maya to the familiarity and security of a well-known cage. This imprisoning physical environment, like the prisons holding both Malcolm X and Eldridge Cleaver, becomes a literal metaphor for her spiritual imprisonment. At the nadir of her quest for selfhood, she climbs readily back in, losing herself in her silent world, surrendering herself to her own ugliness and worthlessness: "The barrenness of Stamps was exactly what I wanted, without will or consciousness" (86).

III

Maya lives in solitude for one year until the lovely Mrs. Flowers walks into her grandmother's store and comes to play the role for Maya that Beverly Axelrod plays for Cleaver. It is Mrs. Flowers who opens the door to the caged bird's silence with the key of loving acceptance. For the first time, Maya is accepted as an individual rather than as a relation to someone else. Her identity is self-generated rather than derivative: "I was liked, and what a difference it made. I was respected not as Mrs. Henderson's grandchild or Bailey's sister but for just being Marguerite Johnson" (98). Such unqualified acceptance allows her to experience the incipient power of her own self-worth.

But while a consciousness of her own self-worth germinates inside her, outside, in the life that revolves around her, hovers the stagnant air of impotence and frustration. And precisely because she has always remained an outsider to the way of life in Stamps and precisely because she is beginning to feel the power of her own selfhood, Maya gradually becomes conscious of such powerlessness. The older autobiographer recalls vividly specific moments illustrative of such powerlessness: the evening Bailey comes home later than usual and Maya watches her grandmother worry, "her heartstrings tied to a hanging noose"; the church meeting during which she comes to realize that her neighbors used religion as a way of "bask[ing] in the righteousness of the poor and the exclusiveness of the downtrodden." Even the Joe Louis fight, which sends a thrill of pride through a black community vicariously winning victory over a white man (the white community), becomes a grotesque counterpoint to the normal way of life. Then at the graduation ceremony, during the exciting expectations of the young graduates and their families and friends are exploded casually by the words of an oblivious and insensitive white speaker, who praises the youths for being promising athletes and indirectly reminds them all that they are destined to be "maids and farmers, handy-

men and washerwomen," the young girl comes to understand fully the desperation of impotence: "It was awful to
be Negro and have no control over my life. It was brutal to
be young and already trained to sit quietly and listen to
charges brought against my color with no chance of defense. We should all be dead" (176). Finally, when Maya
and her grandmother make an humiliating attempt to see a
white dentist who refuses them, informing them cursorily
that he would "rather stick [his] hand in a dog's mouth than
in a nigger's," the child finds compensation for her impotence the only way she can—by fantasizing that her grandmother has ordered the white dentist to leave town and that
he actually obeys her.

One gesture, however, foreshadows Maya's eventual inability to sit quietly and is very much an expression of her
growing acceptance of her own self-worth. For a short time,
she works in the house of Mrs. Viola Cullinan, but for a
short time only, for Mrs. Cullinan, with an easiness that
comes from long tradition, assaults her ego by calling her
Mary rather than Maya. This oversight, offered so casually,
is a most devastating sign of the black girl's invisibility in
white society. In failing to call her by her name, the symbol
of her uniqueness, Mrs. Cullinan fails to respect her humanity. Maya understands this perfectly and rebels by
breaking Mrs. Cullinan's most cherished dish. The black
girl is assuming the consciousness of the rebel as the stance
necessary for preserving her individuality and affirming
her self-worth.

But now there is yet another move, to wartime San Francisco. Here in this big city everything seems out of place:
"The air of collective displacement, the impermanence of
life in wartime and the gauche personalities of the more
recent arrivals tended to dissipate my own sense of not
belonging. In San Francisco, for the first time, I perceived

myself as part of something" (205). Maya had been on the move when she entered Stamps and thus could not settle into its rigid way of life. She chose to remain an outsider and, in so doing, chose not to allow her personality to become rigidified. The fluidity of her new environment, however, matches the fluidity of her physical, psychological, and intellectual life. She feels in place in an environment where everyone and everything seem out of place.

Even more significant than the total displacement of San Francisco is Maya's trip to Mexico with her father. The older autobiographer, in giving form to her past experience, discovers that this moment was a turning point in her quest after authentic selfhood. Maya accompanies her father to a small Mexican town where he proceeds to get obliviously drunk, leaving her with the responsibility of getting them back to Los Angeles by car, although she had never driven one. For the first time, Maya finds herself totally in control of her situation. Her new sense of power contrasts vividly with her former despair that as a Negro she has no control over her fate.

Then, when Maya and her father return home, an argument between Maya and her stepmother Dolores ensues: Dolores calls Maya's mother a whore; Maya slaps her; Dolores cuts her severely with a knife; Maya's father rushes Maya to a friend's house and leaves her. Because she fears a scene of violence if she returns to her mother, who would certainly discover the wounds, Maya runs away and finds a new home in a wrecked car in a junkyard. Here among a community of homeless youths, "the silt of war frenzy," she lives for a month and discovers warmth, acceptance, security, brotherhood.

These experiences provide Maya with a knowledge of self-mastery and a confirmation of self-worth. With the assumption of this power, she is ready to challenge the unwritten, restrictive social codes of San Francisco. Mrs. Cullinan's broken dish prefigures the struggle for her job on the streetcar as the first black money collector. Stamps' acquiescence is left far behind as Maya assumes control over her own social destiny and engages in the struggle with life's forces. She has broken through the rusted bars of her social cage.

But Maya must still break open the bars of her female sexuality. Although she now feels power over her social identity, she feels insecurity about her sexual identity. She remains the embarrassed child who stands before the Easter congregation asking, "What you looking at me for?" The bars of her physical being close in on her, threatening her peace of mind. The lack of femininity in her small-breasted, straight-lined, hairless physique and the heaviness of her voice become, in her imagination, symptomatic of latent lesbian tendencies. A gnawing self-consciousness plagues her. Even after her mother's amused knowledge disperses her fears, the mere fact of her attraction to a classmate's breasts undermines any confidence that reassurance had provided: it was only brief respite against her fears. The only remedy available to her seems to be a heterosexual liaison. But even making love with a casual male acquaintance fails to quell her suspicions; the whole affair is an unenjoyable experience.

Only her pregnancy provides a climactic reassurance that she is indeed a heterosexual woman: if she can become pregnant, she certainly cannot be a lesbian (a specious argument in terms of logic but a compelling one in terms of the emotions and psychology of a young girl). The birth of the baby brings Maya something totally her own. More important, it brings her to a recognition and acceptance of her full, instinctual womanhood. The child, father to the

woman, opens the caged door and allows the fully developed woman to fly out. Now she feels the control of her
sexual identity as well as her social identity. The girl child
no longer need ask, embarrassed, "What you looking at me
for?" No longer need she fantasize any other reality than
her own. Like Cleaver, the black man, she has gained physical, intellectual, and spiritual self-mastery.

Maya Angelou's autobiography comes to a sense of an
ending: the black American girl child has succeeded in
freeing herself from the natural and social bars imprisoning her in the cage of her own diminished self-image by
assuming control of her life and fully accepting her black
womanhood. The displaced child has found a "place." With
the birth of her child, Maya is herself born into a mature
engagement with the forces of life. In welcoming that
struggle, she refuses to live a death of quiet acquiescence:
"Few, if any, survive their teens. Most surrender to the
vague but murderous pressure of adult conformity. It becomes easier to die and avoid conflicts than to maintain a
constant battle with the superior forces of maturity" (231).

IV

One way of dying to life's struggle is to suppress its
inevitable pain by forgetting the past. Maya Angelou successfully banished the memories of past years to the unconscious where they lay dormant while she continued on to
her years of dance and drama, of writing in Africa and in
New York. She specifically alludes to this loss when in the
acknowledgments she thanks her editor at Random House,
"who gently prodded me back into the lost years." To the
extent that these years were lost, a part of herself was lost.
Once she accepted the challenge of recovering them, she
accepted the challenge of rediscovering and thus reaffirm-

ing her own selfhood. Maya Angelou, like Richard Wright, comes to understand more fully who she is by remembering who she has been and how she came to be who she is. Unlike a large number of black autobiographers who have achieved a sense of freedom in the achievement of fame, Maya Angelou chooses not to focus on the traditional success story of her life but rather on the adolescence that shaped her and prepared her for those later achievements.

Moreover, she makes the journey back into her past in its own terms by immersing herself once again in the medium of her making. Stamps, Arkansas, imprinted its way of life on the child during her formative years: the lasting evidence of this imprint is the sound of it. Maya Angelou's vitality and genius as a writer lies in her acute sensitivity to the sound of the life around her, in her ability to recapture the texture of the way of life in the texture of its rhythms, its idioms, its idiosyncratic vocabulary, and especially its process of image making. This ability is a product of several factors in her past experience. First of all, she entered Stamps as an outsider, which gave her a conscious ear for all that was said and done around her. She was not born into the life; she adopted it, and to do so most effectively involved learning and then adopting its language. Then, when her experience with Mr. Freeman sent her into a hibernation of silence, she read even more avidly than before and always continued to do so. Her desire to read was by and large a need to fantasize a more ideal existence, a more ideal self.

> To be allowed, no, invited, into the private lives of strangers, and to share their joys and fears, was a chance to exchange the Southern bitter wormwood for a cup of mead with Beowulf or a hot cup of tea and milk with Oliver Twist. When I said aloud, "It is a far, far

better thing that I do, than I have ever done . . ." tears
of love filled my eyes at my selflessness. (97)

And also Mrs. Flowers, her surrogate mother, taught her
certain "lessons of living," one of which had directly to do
with Maya's sensitivity to the language of Stamps:

> She said I must always be intolerant of ignorance but
> understanding of illiteracy. That some people, unable
> to go to school, were more educated and even more
> intelligent than college professors. She encouraged me
> to listen carefully to what country people called mother
> wit. That in those homely sayings was couched the
> collective wisdom of generations. (97)

The "collective wisdom of generations" is part of what
shaped Maya Angelou's identity. That she chooses to recreate the past in its own sounds suggests that she accepts
the past and recognizes its beauty and its ugliness, its
strengths and its weaknesses. In *I Know Why the Caged Bird
Sings,* not only does the black girl child struggle successfully
for the freedom of self-worth; the black self also returns to
and accepts the past in the return to and full acceptance of
its language, a symbolic construct of a way of life. The
liabilities inherent in the way of life are transformed
through the agency of art into a positive force.

Notes

[1]Maya Angelou, *I Know Why the Caged Bird Sings,* p. 5. Further
citations will appear in the text.

[2]William H. Grier and Price M. Cobbs, *Black Rage,* p. 40.

7

LOSS

"I'm not at home any place or with anyone."
—Horace Cayton, Long Old Road

Eldridge Cleaver's autobiography, like that of Malcolm X, attests to the continual possibilities for rebirth open to the black self at the same time that it dramatizes the heroic possibilities of racial leadership inherent in Malcolm X's drama of selfhood. Literally imprisoned, the black self discovers, through the process of self-conscious analysis, real freedom in its public role as the new mythical black hero and revolutionary prophet. However, Cleaver's autobiography also reveals a multifarious self composed of interchangeable masks responsive to a particular mood or to a particular occasion. This protean quality manifest in Soul On Ice *portends certain negative possibilities inherent in any public role and reintroduces the theme of masking. As I noted earlier, the fabrication of the mask served two positive functions for the slave: it was a defensive or passive weapon of survival and an offensive or aggressive weapon of manipulation, to be used for a cause or for self-aggrandizement.*

Cleaver himself is conscious of the manipulative propensity of the mask, a fact that renders him a potential, if not at times a real, con man. He is aware that he is a master of disguise and that disguise is effectively employed for the manipulation of a public. After the schism between Elijah Muhammad and Malcolm X, for example, he rejects the Muslim's black nationalism and racism, admitting that "a rebirth does not follow automatically." Then he goes on to reveal a con man's facility with protean disguises by refashioning a new "vision": "I have tried a tentative compromise by adopting a select vocabulary, so that now when I see the whites of their eyes, instead of saying "devil" or "beast" I say "imperialist" or "capitalist," and everyone seems to be happier" (66). Later, in his first letter to Beverly Axelrod, he displays his protean nature as he becomes in turn confused lover, exaggerator, humble egotist, accuser, ironist, hater, dead man bereft of an identity, and finally, the con man revealed and revelling in his roles:

NOW TURN THE RECORD OVER AND PLAY THE OTHER SIDE

I have tried to mislead you. I am not humble at all. I have no humility and I do not fear you in the least. If I pretend to be shy, if I appear to hesitate, it is only a sham to deceive. By playing the humble part, I sucker my fellow men in and seduce them of their trust. And then, if it suits my advantage, I lower the boom—mercilessly. I lied when I stated that I had no sense of myself. I am very well aware of my style. My vanity is as vast as the scope of a dream, my heart is that of a tyrant, my arm is the arm of the executioner. It is only the failure of my plots that I fear. Whereas in the past we have had Prophets of Doom, in my vanity I wish to be the Voice of Doom itself. I am angry at the insurgents of Watts. They have pulled the covers off me and revealed to all what potential may lie behind my Tom Smile. (144)

The con man, responsive to his victims' vulnerabilities, reshapes his public identity in order to manipulate the public and ensure his goal. Since Cleaver's role is a public one, the tactics of the con man are one means of capturing an audience and ultimately accomplishing his goal. This is not to imply that conscious manipulation is Cleaver's only or even central impulse. In fact, he expressly intends not to be, on the whole, deceptive. His aim is to expose the corruption of society by direct rather than indirect means: "I think all of us, the entire nation, will be better off if we bring it all out front" (17). "All out front" is exactly where the con man does not bring it. Cleaver attempts to unmask the truth, to destroy the fantasies and illusions plaguing American society, and, in so doing, to enlighten society and thus precipitate change.

Any use of masking is nevertheless fraught with ambiguous moral and psychic possibilities, the most negative of which are best dramatized in Ellison's Invisible Man through the introduction of Rinehart, the master of disguises and a pure representative of the con man type, the individual who manipulates public identities to attain his own selfish ends. When Ellison's protagonist is mistaken for Rinehart, he is initiated into the world of infinite roles and, in response, asks himself:

> Could he be all of them: Rine the runner and Rine the gambler and Rine the briber and Rine the lover and Rinehart the Reverend? Could he himself be both rind and hart? What is real anyway? But how could I doubt it? He was a broad man, a man of parts who got around. Rinehart the rounder. It was true as I was true. His world was possibility and he knew it. . . . A vast seething, hot world of fluidity, and Rine the rascal was at home in it. (376)

Rinehart's identities are as numerous as the infinite possibilities of his masks. But if he is thus the rind, or the outside, public role, can he be also the hart, or the inside, private self? If the self's identity is a composite of its public masks, asks the protagonist, "What on earth was hiding behind the face of things? If dark glasses and a white hat could blot out my identity so quickly, who actually was who?" (373).

The other side of the coin of possibility is chaos or nothingness. If the self can be whoever it wants to be, it may be, in fact, nothing—all rind and no hart.

This potential "nothingness" behind the self's roles is the most nihilistic, the most negative, ramification of the act of masking. There is, however, another negative ramification not quite so devastatingly nihilistic: the embrace of a public role or mask may be a form of escape from the private self. Ellison's invisible man goes underground with the realization that every social role is a mask that obscures the private self. When he becomes famous as a leader of the Brotherhood, people he does not know greet him, causing him to become aware

> *that there were two of me: the old self that slept a few hours a night and dreamed sometimes of my grandfather and Bledsoe and Brockway and Mary, the self that flew without wings and plunged from great heights; and the new public self that spoke for the brotherhood and was becoming so much more important than the other that I seemed to run a foot race against myself.* (330)

Immersion in a public cause, a public role, may result in legitimate self-fulfillment as it does for Malcolm X and Cleaver. But it is equally possible that the public self may alienate the individual from his private self; immersion in a public role may be, in fact, an escape from the self, a possibility embodied in Horace Cayton's autobiography, Long Old Road.

I

Horace Cayton's journey to public leadership and private emptiness originates in his ancestral past with which, appropriately, the autobiography begins:

Four disparate people—an ex-slave, a United States Senator, a wisp of a mulatto Quaker girl, and a proud white plantation owner's daughter—were my grandparents. Each has had an influence on me and my family. My father's father had been proud and courageous, refusing to be held down by caste or class proscriptions. Born and raised a slave, he ended as a prosperous, independent farmer who provided my father with an education and the desire to escape the southland. My mother's father became a symbol of achievement for all Negroes by achieving the highest position a Negro had ever held in the history of our country. My Quaker grandmother maintained a cultured home from which my mother took her inspiration and which had forged religious steel into my mother's character. And the white woman, who was my grandmother and whose name I never knew, made us aware that all man-made barriers are penetrable; for the blood of the masters flowed in our veins.

Each had in his or her way rebelled, and all except the lonely white woman had succeeded. We, unlike most Negroes, lived in a tradition of success, achievement, and no hope for Negro liberation. With such sterling examples to guide us, surrender to prejudice seemed cowardly and unnecessary. Our goals were dictated by our past; we were obligated by our family history to achievement in our fight for individual and racial equality.[1]

Cayton's inheritance contrasts sharply with the inheritances of the slave narrator and Booker T. Washington for, unlike these earlier autobiographers, he is willed a firm sense of identity through an ancestral legacy that predetermines his life's journey to a certain extent. His autobiography is a story not of gain but of loss.

A successful, wealthy, and respected member of the middle-class Seattle community, the Cayton family represents the highest achievement of American democratic possibilities promised by emancipation, an achievement Cayton's father reaffirms when Booker T. Washington visits Seattle and stays with the family:

> "Here in the Northwest we are striking out in every direction. Negroes in this town have become small businessmen or skilled mechanics and live a good life. Their children are getting education and will be able to stand up and compete with other men. Here the race is to the swiftest, and here the American dream is being won. I believe in this country very much, Dr. Washington; I believe in it and I love it. I believe in democracy. And here democracy is being worked out. We are the new frontier, and thousands of Negroes come to this part of the country and stand up like men and compete with their white brothers. And those who stay in the South should carry on a relentless fight for their freedom down there." (20)

Long Old Road, therefore, commences with the apparent freedom of assimilation: the Caytons are active participants in the American drama of success. But the moment of shattering disillusionment in black autobiography seems inescapable. In reality, the basis of assimilation is fragile, the legacy of slavery so persistent as to erupt threateningly. A newspaper misquotes the name of Mrs. Cayton's club for Negro improvement: the Dorcus Charity Club becomes the Darky's Charity Club. In addition, latent fears of trespassing the codes of black-white relationships, retained from slave days, surface: the night Cayton's father strikes a white man, the family takes refuge in the darkened basement. The "radical break," one not, like that of the slave narrator, from slavery to freedom but, like that of Hughes and Malcolm X, from the illusory freedom of assimilation to the real imprisonment of a social identity, is forced upon the Cayton family when the social situation in Seattle undergoes a gradual change that fatally affects its status. Horace's father chooses to speak out against the brutal lynching of a southern black, and, as a result, his newspaper subscriptions from white readers fall drastically, driving his paper out of business. By choosing to assert himself, the black courts self-destruction; by demanding visibility, he discovers his own social invisibility. Moreover, the Caytons, no longer one of the few black families in their community, melt into the great mass of blacks emigrating northward and thereby lose their individuality. The American dream of democratic possibility proves once again to be merely a myth for the black man.

Coincident with the Cayton family's fall is young Horace's own journey into total alienation, a result of that very attempt to assimilate. Because the Cayton children have been brought up to consider themselves no one's inferior, they are unprepared for and therefore mystified by the reality they confront outside the home. Again, as elsewhere in black autobiography, this difference is expressed through the rite of naming. Inside the home, the mother's maiden name, "Revels," represents a whole concept of reality for the Cayton children, whose maternal grandfather had been a United States Senator—the reality of assimilation and achievement; but, Cayton writes, "I was quick to learn that a senator grandfather would get me nowhere outside our home" (12), for outside the home, "nigger" represents the reality of their social imprisonment. He tells his sister Madge:

> "I don't know what to do when they call me that. I know I'm not supposed to like it but I don't know why. I asked Mother once and she said that I wasn't a nigger and just to call them nigger back because they were the real niggers. But it doesn't work. They just laugh and say they aren't niggers and that I am." (13)

He confronts the real extent of his alienation from the white community when he attempts to play with Nelly, a young white neighbor whose mother sends him home, warning him never to return: "That was my first attempt to enter the fairyland of the whites; and it had failed mercilessly" (17). In his effort to play with Nelly, Horace rejects his own brother Revels, who sits and broods on the curb, a pattern of behavior repeated later when he rejects the only black girl at school in order to dance with his white schoolmates. This pattern of rejection has been, in fact, an integral part of his upbringing, for, before their fall, his parents had maintained a household that, in looking toward white middle-class culture, completely shunned lower-class black culture and thereby alienated the Cayton children from the very community that offered them any real possibility of acceptance. As a result, he cannot gain entrance to the black community because he is unable to play the black role: he does not know how to act—"what to say, how to dress, what language to employ" (34). In spite of himself, Cayton does not know how to wear the mask that would gain him access to the black community and redress from the white community, a mask that would have guaranteed his survival as a black in a white world.

Thus, assimilation breeds an intense alienation that faces, like Wright's, in two directions—toward black society as well as white society. Suspended in a no-man's land—looking upward to the white world that beckons at the same time that it denies acceptance, looking downward at the black world that repulses at the same time that it carries the only possibility for acceptance—Cayton becomes an outsider or, in his own words, a "cornered rat," who consequently chooses to rebel by challenging the unwritten codes of theatre seating. His father, who appreciates Horace's rebellious nature, recognizes at the same time that it needs redirecting. First, he advises Horace that he cannot separate himself from the black community; second, he suggests that Horace prepare for effective rebellion by getting an education. The legacy of his ancestors demands that Horace participate in the life-long struggle for freedom.

But Horace does not have patience. Youth is too impulsive; it demands immediate results. The legacy is forgotten temporarily as he rebels unilaterally through flight, running first to a position on a ship traveling the northwest coast. Here Horace is temporarily relieved of the tension resulting from his tenuous place in society, for on shipboard the caste system is rigid: "My position was fixed by the laws and traditions of the sea; I could not rise to a higher status nor could I lose my position" (41). The community of the ship is a microcosmic society in which everyone knows his place, in which no dreams of advancement clash with reality, no fears of demotion threaten. Like the southern black who, finding the fluidity of the North unsettling, returns South to the fixed social codes, Cayton welcomes this security. But his respite is short-lived: the ship is, after all, only a ship, not society. Back in Seattle, he is again unable to find a place for himself in society and finally, motivated by his alienation and loneliness, resorts to crime, a pattern which recapitulates that of Malcolm X and Cleaver. With his return from reform school, he is still an outcast of the family, an alienated black youth who drifts from job to job, strike-breaking, courting and then rejecting unions, and finally shipping out again on boats traveling the West Coast. Cayton is a running man who unlike the slave narrator, lacks direction.

This directionless running culminates in a crucial "turning point" when, as a boat steward, Horace overhears the conversation between a naked white woman whose room he has been cleaning and her male companion who returns as the youth leaves:

> "Were you parading around naked in front of that coon, you little slut?"
> "Do you mind?" she asked. "It gave him a thrill and it amused me. What's the difference what the little nigger saw?" (122)

Later as he narrates the experience to a friend, he describes it as an assault on his manhood.

> "Oh, she's pretty, all right. But the way she treated me—like I was a stick, like I had no manhood. She even asked me to powder her back. And when I left she told her husband, or whoever he is, that it *amused* her. A servant isn't supposed to be a man, especially if he's colored—just an animal or something. First I was startled, then I was excited. Now I'm mad." (122)

Cayton's emasculation emanates from his invisibility as a black man and, as a result, finds its ramification in hatred for blacks and hatred, ultimately, for himself, a hatred to which he admits when he takes his brother Revels to the legitimate theater and afterward, swept away from reality in the dream world of the stage, confesses:

> "I just can't go back to the ship, Revs. . . . I hate it—it's dirty and rotten. I'm going to get out of it. I hate those black niggers I have to work with. . . . I hate niggers, especially after seeing that show. Don't you hate being a nigger and having to sleep in a filthy glory hole?"
>
> "You shouldn't talk like that, bubba. . . . It's disloyal to our people. Do you want to be white?"
>
> "Not exactly, I met some pretty lousy white people on the boats. I wouldn't want to be like them. I just want to be free."
>
> "But then you wouldn't be either white or colored. What would you be? Where would you go to church?"
>
> I became disturbed about what I'd said, guilty about my disloyalty to Negroes. "Rev, I didn't mean that I would go back on our race. I'll always fight for them. But I hate the way colored people have to live. Negroes are treated so bad that I sometimes hate them, even myself, for being a Negro." (124-125)

Cayton, enslaved by white society, is more dramatically imprisoned in his own self-hatred, his own ambiguous sense of identity. Like the slave narrator when still a slave, he yearns for freedom; but the slave narrator could equate freedom with northern society while Cayton is already in that society. At this point, therefore, the youth must begin again, seek a new way to escape.

Education becomes the new road to apparent freedom as Cayton finishes high school, college, and continues on to graduate school. Through the study of sociology he finds identification with the greater black community, an identification Cleaver finds through his study of politics, economics, and history and Malcolm X through his religion. In contrast with his early experiences, which alienated him completely from the black community and suspended him in a no-man's land, this new experience inspires him to re-enter that community and to seek self-fulfillment through his own public role as leader. Nevertheless, as a graduate student in Chicago, he is still unable to gain acceptance in the black community: an intellectual, he is alienated from the masses; a graduate student, he is separated from the black undergraduate students; a student, he is unwelcomed by the wealthy black business and professional class. He is confined to membership in the community of graduate students and young faculty, by and large a white one. Frustrated, he again takes to flight. He runs to the South, to the black community of Tuskegee, but the inability of the school to understand the needs and frustrations of blacks who desire to leave for the North is unacceptable to Cayton, who feels again "like an alien in a strange country" (205). He runs onward to Europe only to realize that, although he may be an outsider in his own country, he is a foreigner in any other. He runs back to America still lonely, still alienated, still a man without a community.

A year at Fisk, a second marriage, this time to a black woman, and residence in the black belt of Chicago, however, soon place him squarely within the black community. The height of his public achievement comes when he co-authors *Black Metropolis* and, thereafter, becomes recognized as a "race leader" and "race man":

A race leader was expected to put up some sort of aggressive resistance against the exclusion and subordination of Negroes; more specifically, in Chicago at that time, it meant protesting against the job ceiling

and the black ghetto. I was active in every fight for
Negro rights and spoke at churches, white and black, at
forums, before civic and governmental bodies. I also
served on numerous committees. But besides being a
race leader, I also became a race man. Frustrated by
their isolation from the mainstream of American life
and out of their impotence to control their fate deci-
sively, Negroes developed the notion of a race man, an
individual who was proud of his race and always tried
to uphold it whether it was good or bad, right or wrong.
Perhaps in an ardent attempt to live down my past, to
make up for having married white and for having so
many white friends, I found it necessary to become a
race man, even a dedicated one. (250)

Malcolm X and Cleaver find self-fulfillment in their public
roles as race leaders and race men; so ostensibly does
Cayton. He has stopped running from the black community and runs, instead, to a place within that community, to
the "home" for which he has been searching. His ancestral
mission has apparently been fulfilled. Yet the self-criticism
of the passage above intimates that the assumption of a
public role of leadership has, in fact, been another form of
escape, an escape from latent self-hatred and private am-
bivalences, an escape, therefore, from the private self.
Ellison's invisible man, as his fame as a community leader
spreads, finds his public and private selves in conflict, with
the result that the public self gains ascendancy. Cayton
experiences this same split:

I had at last succeeded in becoming an important person among Negroes. But I had done so at great cost, for
although outwardly I was established I had not really

found my own identity. This search was to haunt my existence and provide an inner conflict which I would endure for the rest of my days. (254)

As a leader, he has unwittingly sacrificed his private self to his public role, unlike Malcolm X and Cleaver who do so consciously and who, in losing themselves to that role, paradoxically, gain themselves. Cayton's loss of self in his role as leader has been precisely that—a loss of self, an escape from identity.

The devastating awareness one night that he cannot love sends Cayton to the psychoanalyst to explore this private alienation. In confessing his unmitigated hatred of white people to the analyst, he develops his concept of the hate-fear-hate complex, which characterizes the psychic conflict of the black in America: "The Negro has been hurt; he knows it. He wants to strike back, but he must not—there is evidence everywhere that to do so may lead to his destruction" (265). Such repressed hatred becomes a form of self-destruction, one that Malcolm X and Cleaver transform into their revolutionary programs as they project that hatred outward upon society rather than inward, as they do battle with society rather than the self, but one that Cayton cannot or does not redirect. Thus, his hatred and anger are internalized; internalized, they become so self-destructive that eventually chaos engulfs him. With the explosion of the atomic bomb on Japan, Cayton feels open disloyalty to the United States, who chooses to drop the bomb on the yellow rather than the white enemy. His identities—as American and Negro—conflict, driving him to physical and mental collapse. Totally confused, he travels to Woodstock to buy a statue of a nude female by the sculptor Archipenko, drunkenly dubbing his journey a quest after the Holy Grail; in so doing, he transforms the geographical journey into a spiritual one. The statue, a figure of the Virgin Mary, promises him peace and rebirth, but, symbolically, he drops it soon after purchasing it and watches as it breaks in two. Since the statue assumes a symbolic meaning for him, his failure to carry it safely and derive peace from it presages his own subsequent breakdown.

Characteristic of black autobiography, Cayton suffers a physical breakdown symbolic of his spiritual torment: "In the five years following the war, my world collapsed; events piled up in a disorderly fashion, shaking my confidence and leaving me stripped of the will to continue" (309). His job is unsatisfactory, his mother and sister die, his brother rejects him; these events destroy family ties. Then the death of twelve blacks in a fire and his frustrating participation on the board of inquiry completely erase his hopes of Negro improvement: "Why any longer strive to be a leader in this unequal, futile fight for equality?" (327). When his public role as leader, his only means of self-definition becomes meaningless, he is deprived of any sense of self. This descent to nonidentity reaches its nadir when, in Pittsburgh to visit the editor of the *Courier,* he loses the last vestige of identity—his name. Attempting to make a telephone call he "realize[s] with horror that [he] didn't know who [he] was" (343). Cayton's journey reverses the pattern of the slave narrator: the slave narrator sought a new name symbolic of his rebirth into a free identity; Cayton, in contrast, loses or gives up his name, symbolic of his loss of identity. If Cleaver's role as black leader transforms him into the heroic black self, Cayton's failure in his role as leader transforms him into an antiheroic black self. Any public role, as Ellison implies, is a mask that may only compound the self's alienation from its own "hart." Like the invisible man, who escapes underground after his recognition of his identity,

Cayton takes refuge in the quasi-underground existence of the drunkard and bum.

Cayton's illness is an illness of self-hatred: "Perhaps I hate myself more than I hate anything else," he later tells the young Swedish girl whom he almost marries. Moreover, his illness betrays a lack of at-homeness:

> My illness is a sickness of the soul, something beyond religion or psychiatry. It's the sickness of the age. It's a form of alienation—or better, the result of alienation. It's a loss of identity, a lack of at-homeness. I'm not at home in any place or with anyone. (380)

Every avenue of escape has returned Cayton, a modern slave, to the chains of nonidentity. His assumption of a public role as black leader in fulfillment of his ancestral legacy has only been an attempt to escape the confusion of his private self and has therefore, in the end, failed: "I had no identity, but I could no longer afford to risk destroying myself trying to provide one for every other Negro" (400).

The pattern of Cayton's autobiographical experience, in contrast to that of Malcolm X and Eldridge Cleaver, poses the alternative possibility that any assumption of a public identity—in this instance based solely on racial identity —results in a destructive sacrifice of self. A public role may, in fact, be an escape from private identity, for the role automatically predetermines the self's identity; the self does not create itself from within. Cayton's autobiography, a reverse slave narrative, traces the black self's journey into alienation and dissolution rather than to freedom.

II

To be unaware of form, or identity, is, according to

Ellison's protagonist, "to live a death." Cayton's autobiography, in contrast to those of Cleaver, Angelou, and Malcolm X, concludes not with the discovery of a new, authentic identity but with the mere decision to "live" rather than
continue his deathlike existence. Cayton, therefore, comes
out from underground in order to discover his identity.
That discovery is, of course, the beginning of a new journey
to the freedom of the promised land: "When I discover who
I am, I'll be free" (185), realizes the invisible man.

Cayton associates this act of discovery explicitly with the
process of writing an autobiography: "I'm only sure of one
thing: I'm going to write—about myself. Maybe if I put it all
on paper I'll see who I am" (399). In fact, Cleaver, Angelou,
and Cayton have all recognized and reaffirmed the curative
power of the act of writing autobiography. After becoming
a rapist, Cleaver loses his manhood and self-respect; his
"whole fragile moral structure seemed to collapse, completely shattered." "To save [him]self" he begins to write;
the composition of the essays and letters, through which he
discovers his public identity as mythical black hero and
revolutionary prophet, helps to awaken this Lazarus from a
death-in-life existence and to restore his full manhood.
Angelou rediscovers lost years and thus part of herself.
Cayton, too, recognizes that he "must go through some sort
of personal catharsis": "Perhaps in the writing of the book I
might at last find myself" (400-401). Engulfed in the chaos
of nonidentity, stranded in the no-man's-land of total
metaphysical alienation, Cayton seeks release from the oppression of his past and finds a possible road to freedom in
the act of recreating that past. By imposing the patterned
order of art on the chaos of past experience, the autobiographer discovers his identity by discovering some sense of
rootedness, continuity, coherence, unity. By way of gaining

mastery over that past, he creates himself, and, by creating himself, he frees himself. Thus, Cleaver, Angelou, and Cayton pose yet another possibility for the escape from imprisonment to the freedom of an authentic identity.

Notes

[1] Horace Cayton, *Long Old Road,* pp. 2-3. Further citations will appear in the text.

8

CREATIVE

TRANSCENDENCE

"Every man's got to pick his own time to stop running."
—*Claude Brown,* Manchild in the Promised Land

"Run!"
"Where?"

The first exclamation of Claude Brown's Manchild in the
Promised Land *echoes the slave narrative of more than a century
ago. The second summarizes in one word the dilemma that has
characterized the contemporary black self's search for the freedom of
an authentic identity. William Wells Brown and his contemporaries never had to ask "Where?" when they ran: they knew a
"free" self lay to the North. But after emancipation, American
society continued to imprison the black in a social identity that
forbade legitimate self-assertion. In response, the black self could,
like Booker T. Washington, choose to wear a mask and play the role
that would insure his acceptance and even prominence, or he could,
like Wright and others of the migrant generation—including
Claude Brown's own parents—refuse to be enslaved by a social*

mask and again journey northward to the "promised land" as the slave had earlier.

Because of the great and continuing black migration, the North continued to function as a potential symbol of freedom. However, as the experiences of Langston Hughes, Malcolm X, Horace Cayton, and Brown's parents dramatize, this generation was ultimately a disillusioned one. But what of the next? In his prologue, Brown describes the difference between the generation of migrators and their children. Whereas the older one is disillusioned, the younger is desperate: "To add to their misery, they had little hope of deliverance. For where does one run to when he's already in the promised land?" [1]

Because geographical escape is no longer a viable possibility, the black self is thrown back on its own resources and forced to discover an interior escape route from imprisonment to freedom. Malcolm X and Eldridge Cleaver freed themselves by being reborn into full black manhood, Maya Angelou into full black womanhood. Moreover, Malcolm X and Cleaver channel that recovered manhood into a social identity within the black community. Cayton, on the other hand, discovered the negative possibilities of such a social identity: immersion in a public role ultimately returned him to the chains of nonidentity. However, another possibility emerges: both Cayton and Cleaver recognize the positive possibilities for the self's escape through the act of writing itself. Freedom comes through artistic confrontation. Claude Brown's autobiography embodies this very possibility, presenting this study's final thematic and stylistic approach to the black self's search for identity.

I

Thematically, *Manchild in the Promised Land* recapitulates the motifs of the slave narrative and the autobiographies already discussed. What previously were the harsh realities of the plantation are transferred to that larger and more

deadly plantation, the ghetto. There are no direct over-
seers; instead, the overseer is now the greater society surrounding the ghetto, forcing it into self-destructive patterns of existence. *Manchild* is an exposé of the slave system
of the North as the slave narrative and Wright's *Black Boy*
were exposés of the slave system of the South. Brown, like
his predecessor William Wells Brown, vividly portrays the
brutal reality of life in Harlem. The opening incident suggests the imprisoning fabric of Harlem life by introducing
the motifs that will recur again and again. The characteristic reactions to "Sonny Boy's" fate—his being shot in an
attempt to escape the scene of his crime—typify the relationships of Brown to his family and to Harlem society at
large. Walsh, the owner of the fish-and-chips shop into
which Claude flees, shoves the wounded child onto the
floor because he assumes Brown is joking. Such casual,
unconscious cruelty reflects an important environmental
quality of ghetto life. His mother reacts emotionally rather
than rationally, and thus ineffectively; in contrast, his
father is cold, impassive. His mother will always be emotional, his father cruelly authoritarian; both lack adequate
understanding of their son. Drugs intrude immediately: his
friends cannot give blood for him since they have taken
narcotics. His girl-friends worry that he is wounded sexu-
ally, thereby introducing the peer group codes of masculinity. Immediately following this scene comes Brown's oneiric
recollection of a Harlem riot. The juxtaposition of a personal experience of violence and a social outburst of violence reinforces the interdependence of individual and
community identity. Brown's struggle throughout his autobiography is a struggle with his relationship to the community that forms him. It is from this contemporary social
imprisonment that the youth seeks escape. Running, as
elsewhere in black autobiography, is the central thematic

motif. The youth eventually ends his literal flight from police—only to enter upon an infinitely more confusing and desperate psychological flight. He runs from Harlem, but he *is* Harlem or, rather, a very real offspring of Harlem; hence, his running is ultimately away from himself just as Cayton's had been. The young "Sonny Boy" bears the oneiric legacy of Ellison's protagonist: "Keep this nigger-boy running."

Imprisoned within a society that fails to allow the individual genuine humanity and more positive and creative forms of self-fulfillment, Brown unconsciously accepts criminality as a means to self-worth. In the first three chapters, until his return from the reform school at Wiltwyck, he runs away from any authority figure—police, father, school—to the community of his peers:

> My friends were all daring like me, tough like me, dirty like me, ragged like me, cursed like me, and had a great love for trouble like me. We took pride in being able to hitch rides on trolleys, buses, taxicabs and in knowing how to steal and fight. We knew that we were the only kids in the neighborhood who usually had more than ten dollars in their pockets. There were other people who knew this too, and that was often a problem for us. Somebody was always trying to shake us down or rob us. This was usually done by the older hustlers in the neighborhood or by storekeepers or cops. At other times, older fellows would shake us down, con us, or Murphy us out of our loot. We accepted this as the ways of life. Everybody was stealing from everybody else. And sometimes we would shake down newsboys and shoeshine boys. So we really had no complaints coming. Although none of my sidekicks was over twelve

years of age, we didn't think of ourselves as kids. The
other kids my age were thought of as kids by me. I felt
that since I knew more about life than they did, I had
the right to regard them as kids. (21-22)

Just as survival on the plantation involved adherence to
certain unwritten codes so does survival in the contemporary black community, whether the southern black community of the young Richard, the Roxbury ghetto of Malcolm X,
or the Harlem of Brown. The impotency characterizing
Brown's relationship to white society is sublimated in his
role as youthful criminal or "bad nigger" through which he
achieves power and respect and derives a sense of belonging and maturity: "It was fighting and stealing that made
me somebody." His power emanates from the fear he inspires in others. While in the Youth House, he finds that

just about everybody on the third floor . . . was scared
of me, and I liked it. This was the first time I had ever
been anyplace where nearly everybody was scared of
me, and before I knew anything, I was liking it. . . . I was
having more fun than I'd ever had in my whole life.
(61)

In reality, Brown's criminal rebellion is motivated by
intense anger deriving from his own overwhelming fear,
always lurking behind the mask of street masculinity and
forcing the youth into patterns of compulsive fearlessness:
"I had been afraid in Harlem all my life. Even though I did
things that people said were crazy—people who thought
that I must not be afraid of anything—I was afraid of almost
everything" (193). And so it is even more appropriate that
he opens his autobiography with the incident he later de-

scribes as "perhaps . . . the most dramatic moment of [his] life . . . the one time in [his] life when [he] was most afraid of dying" (294).

To the extent that he is forced into standardized forms of action and reaction by the street codes, the youth falls victim to them and thus loses control over his life. Recalling his first successful street fight, the autobiographer refers specifically to their rigorous and intractable nature:

> Afterward, if I came by, they'd start saying, "Hey, Sonny Boy, how you doin'?" They'd ask me, "You kick anybody's ass today?" I knew that they admired me for this, and I knew that I had to keep on doing it. This was the reputation I was making, and I had to keep living up to it every day that I came out of the house. Every day, there was a greater demand on me. I couldn't beat the same little boys every day. They got bigger and bigger. I had to get more vicious as the cats got bigger. When the bigger guys started messing with you, you couldn't hit them or give them a black eye or a bloody nose. You had to get a bottle or a stick or a knife. All the other cats out there on the streets expected this of me, and they gave me encouragement. (259)

The compulsion reflected in this passage is the compulsion of the society into which Brown was born, which forces him, apparently a tough or victimizer, into the potentially self-destructive role of the victim. Because the community grants the status and administers the awards, the self's worth is totally in thrall to its sanctions. Thus, as the young Wright had learned only too well, the black community in reaction to its oppressed status in the white community can impose norms of behavior just as rigidly oppressive as the white community by demanding a pre-established identity of those who would survive. Membership in a community requires self-sacrifice to the roles of that community.

Brown does, however, finally become aware of his victimization as he becomes aware of the "change" in Harlem, accentuated by a long absence at Wiltwyck:

> It was exciting being home for the first few days, the first few weeks. Then I don't know what happened, but suddenly it just seemed to be gone. Harlem had changed a lot. Everybody had changed. I had changed too, but in a different way. I was moving away from things. There was no place for me. I felt lonelier in Harlem than I'd felt when I first went to Wiltwyck. I couldn't go back to Wiltwyck—I had been trying to get away from there for years to get back to this. Now it seemed as though "this" wasn't there any more. It really was confusing for a while. (103)

As we have observed so often in black autobiography, the individual's confrontation with his very real spiritual displacement within the community, whether black or white, results in physical illness: "Sometimes I used to get headaches thinking about it. I used to get sick. I couldn't get up." (122) This tension finds immediate, but temporary, release in the repetition of the traditional patterns of behavior: "I'd get Turk, I'd get Tito, I'd get anybody who was around. I'd say, 'C'mon man, let's go pull a score.' It seemed like the only way I could get away" (122). Brown's clipped prose captures the compulsive need for companionship and some kind of action as a means to recover a sense of at-oneness with life in Harlem.

But at-oneness is no longer possible. Circumstance, in this case, absence, severs Brown from his comfortable social role and forces him to acknowledge that nothing is perma-

nent in the life of Harlem. With this realization, he loses his
ability to play his previously well-fitting, unconsciously em-
braced social role. Thus, he is at odds with himself and with
society, aware only that circumstances over which he has no
control are forever changing around him. What Claude
cannot distinguish between in his youth are the two forms
of change—real and apparent. Drugs and the drug generation cause drastic outward change in Harlem patterns, but
the response to drugs is the unchanging response to the
individual's need for social approval. One code of masculinity is merely substituted for another:

> The manhood thing started getting next to cats
> through drugs. I saw it so many times. Young cats
> wanted to take drugs because they used to listen to the
> way the junkies talked, with a drag in their voice. I used
> to see some of the younger cats on the corner trying to
> imitate the junkie drag, that harsh, "Yeah, man" sort of
> thing. . . . The fighting thing didn't seem to be impor-
> tant any more. The only thing that seemed to matter
> now, to my generation in Harlem, was drugs. (261)

What never changes is the repetitious destruction of ghetto
existence, as the autobiographer ultimately comes to understand: "I suppose no one who has ever lived in a Harlem
of the world could ever imagine that it could change so
drastically and yet maintain so much of its old misery"
(402).

The tone and point of view controlling it combine to
create an imaginative correlative of this journey from "in-
siderness" to "outsiderness." Until Brown begins to feel this
alienation and dislocation, the narration is controlled by a
double point of view—that of the youth and that of the

autobiographer describing his younger self. Both points of view are operating in the following passage:

It was Sunday morning. Kids were coming from church with their mothers and fathers, and some people were sick and vomiting on the street. Most of the people were dressed up, and vomit was all over the street near the beer gardens. There was a lot of blood near the beer gardens and all over the sidewalk on Eighth Avenue. This was a real Sunday morning—a lot of blood and vomit everywhere and people all dressed up and going to church. Some of them were all dressed up and sleeping on the sidewalk or sleeping on building stoops. It was all real good to see again, real good. There were the ladies going to church in white dresses and trying real hard not to look at the men standing on the corners cussing and saying fresh things to them— but trying real hard to listen to what the men were saying without looking as if they were hearing it. That man who was all dressed up and sleeping on the sidewalk propped up against the newspaper stand with a smile on his face sure looked happy. I was so happy to see them, to see it, to see it all, to see Harlem again. (51)

As a secure, unself-conscious member of the Harlem community, the youth responds to the vitality and beauty of the Sunday morning scene. The autobiographer, on the other hand, responds with irony and objectivity to the real horror manifest and latent in the scene.

The first part of the narrative is also characterized by a boldly humorous approach to the material. There is the moment when Claude and his friend Toto face a woman judge after being apprehended for theft:

Mrs. Jones, Toto's mother, was standing right next to Toto and me. And Toto was watching her and trying to look pitiful, just like I was. Mama and Mrs. Jones sure did look crazy with their heads going up and down faster and faster as they peeped up at the mean queen from the bottom of their eyes and tried to look as if they knew what she was saying to them. All I knew was that I was supposed to look sorry for what I had done. Toto knew this too, so we were both looking real sorry while our mothers nodded their heads. All the time, I was wishing that I had gotten caught with somebody else, because Toto was too good at looking pitiful. He was so good that he even made me feel sorry for him. After a while, I stopped trying to look sorry and just tried to look like Toto. I sure was glad that Bulldog wasn't there, because he could look more pitiful than anybody I knew without even trying. When he started looking pitiful, he might have made the mean queen think that Toto and I were laughing. (64)

For the youth, life in Harlem is an easy, fun, exciting, unpredictable game. The autobiographer, through the distance he maintains by his use of irony and humor, recreates his earlier self as a fictional character with a life of his own, and in this way remains true to the reality of his boyhood without sentimentalizing it and true to the reality of Harlem as he understands it at the time of writing.

Just prior to his move away from Harlem, the unquestioning responsiveness of the youth, the insider, gives way before the serious, pained questioning of the dislocated, alienated outsider. The world of Harlem is no longer one of excitement, games, challenges, adventures, and codes; it is potentially, if not actually, destructive. The narrator still maintains a certain distance through his objectivity, but the

point of view is more explicitly self-conscious, more un-
ified; the tone is somber. Deaths, murders, shootings, overdoses, prison sentences, whores, pimps, junkies—all crowd
in on Brown and on the reader. Jim Goldie is shot; Butch
"falls off" a roof and dies; Pimp becomes a junkie. Brown
finds himself still trapped in self-destructive patterns. As a
hustler, he must kill a junkie, an act of vengeance decreed
by street codes. Fortunately, the junkie is caught before
Brown is able to find him; but worried that the next time he
will have to kill, he decides he must leave the street life: "At
seventeen, I was ready to retire from it. I'd already had ten
or eleven years at it" (172). The fear that earlier motivated
Brown to embrace these codes now motivates him to self-
awareness and geographical flight from Harlem.

> Fear made me stop and think. I was able to see things
> differently. I had become convinced that two things
> weren't for me: I wasn't going to go to jail, and I wasn't
> going to kill anybody. But I knew I couldn't completely
> sever all ties with Harlem. My family was there, and just
> about all my life was there. I didn't know anybody
> anywhere else. I didn't know anybody in the Village.
> All I knew was that I had to get away. (132)

Brown feels the need for a radical break so common in
black autobiography. However, his running lacks direction:
it is only running *away from* the imprisonment of Harlem.
Thus, his problem is only temporarily solved; for although
this move to Greenwich Village frees him physically from
Harlem, it does not free him spiritually; Harlem remains
his "point of reference." Change of place does not in itself
guarantee freedom or a new identity; it only deprives him
of any sense of community.

In fact, the alternative community, the white world of the

Village, fails him, too, for it does not grant acceptance or equality. Twice he is questioned by police in his own apartment building about whether he actually lives there; only when the white landlord affirms his residence do the police leave. Other incidents there reinforce his invisibility as a black man, especially with regard to work:

> When I worked at the watch repair shop, if I said anything that would indicate that I thought a little of myself, or if I didn't seem grateful ... they all seemed to think that I was being arrogant in some way or another. They all seemed to have the impression that niggers weren't supposed to act like that. They'd think, This nigger's crazy. What kind of Negro is he? Doesn't he know his place? (287)

Brown's dilemma is paradoxical: he is a running man with nowhere to run. If Harlem offers only alienation from black America, the Village offers only more alienation from white America. The painful ending of his love affair with Judy, whose liberal Jewish parents send her away, more forcefully substantiates his isolation. Like Wright and Cayton before him, Claude Brown is alienated from both black and white society.

This prophetic experience sends him on the road again: "The most natural thing to do was to take refuge in Harlem. I was hurt, and I was running home" (354). The third escape route is the road back to his own community where his desperate struggle against the force of circumstance —which is Harlem—finally comes to an end with an existential awareness of the freedom of self-definition. Brown discovers only too painfully, in his unsuccessful attempt to save his brother Pimp from drug addiction, that each individual must assume responsibility for his own fate and is, therefore, his own creator. Freedom is the acceptance of one's self, of one's own choice of fate. It is, thus, the recognition of choice, a truth Brown attests to in the last scene of the autobiography when he meets Reno, an old friend, who tells Brown that he is at home in jail. Brown replies, "Yeah, Reno, it's good that a cat can be so happy in jail. I guess all it takes to be happy in anything is knowin' how to walk with your lot, whatever it is, in life" (412). After they part, Brown continues to muse: "I felt as though I had let him down. I was saying, 'Look, man, we aren't destined. You just bullshitted yourself and messed all up.' But I guess he hadn't, really. He'd just made his choice, and I'd made mine" (413).

Harlem's circumstances are such that the individual may be lost to life's possibilities by being forced to play out self-destructive roles. The horror persists: Tony dies; Pimp goes to prison. But Brown himself survives as do Turk and Danny. Their survival suggests that the individual is not hopelessly enslaved by society if he will recognize his own freedom to choose. For Brown, if the individual acknowledges and accepts the responsibility for his own life, then that life is really his, and he has won the only viable freedom available. To attempt to escape from those circumstances is to be victimized by them. Running, initially a positive or creative response to social imprisonment, now becomes a negative response, since it is an expression of the lack of responsibility for the self: it is, in fact, flight from self. To stop running and to face those circumstances is to be released from bondage and to win the freedom of self-determination. As Turk says to Brown: "I guess that's what this maturity thing is about, growing up and being able to face being what you are" (359). Certainly there are limitations that circumstance imposes upon the individual, but by accepting those very limitations Brown liberates himself from their oppression. The black self is finally free when it does not flee, when it accepts its past and, therefore, its own self-determination. Danny had once told Brown: "Every man's got to pick his own time, Sonny. Every man's got to pick his own time to stop running" (252). Brown finally stops and by doing so achieves a radical breakthrough to identity.

II

In fact, this thematic resolution is fully realized only through the process of writing the autobiography; for Brown has been able to transcend the destructive limitations of his social identity and affirm the creative possibilities of the self only so far as he has been able to free himself from the oppressive memories of his past experience.

The final paragraphs evoke vividly these earliest memories:

> I used to feel that I belonged on the Harlem streets and that, regardless of what I did, nobody had any business to take me off the streets.
>
> I remember when I ran away from shelters, places that they sent me to, here in the city. I never ran away with the thought in mind of coming home. I always ran away to get back to the streets. I always thought of Harlem as home, but I never thought of Harlem as being in the house. To me, home was the streets. I suppose there were many people who felt that. If home was so miserable, the street was the place to be. I wonder if mine was really so miserable, or if it was that there was so much happening out in the street that it made home seem such a dull and dismal place.

When I was very young—about five years old, maybe younger—I would always be sitting out on the stoop. I remember Mama telling me and Carole to sit on the stoop and not to move away from in front of the door. Even when it was time to go up and Carole would be pulling on me to come upstairs and eat, I never wanted to go, because there was so much out there in that street.

You might see somebody get cut or killed. I could go out in the street for an afternoon, and I would see so much that, when I came in the house, I'd be talking and talking for what seemed like hours. Dad would say, "boy, why don't you stop that lyin'? You know you didn't see all that. You know you didn't see nobody do that." But I knew I had. (415)

Brown's final terse, unequivocal concluding statement confirms the reality of this past and is addressed to himself as much as to the reader, for such a past seems too fantastic to be anything but a dream (or a nightmare), a possibility he proposes several times:

I had a funny feeling about everything, about the past, about my childhood, and I kind of wondered if Jackie had been real, if the childhood had been real, if we had all gone through all that stuff. I wondered if it weren't really just a dream. I couldn't understand Bucky's not being around. It just never made sense. I guess you just had to take it as it was. (369)

The act of writing reinvests the past, a dreamlike phantom, with a vivid immediacy, thus verifying its reality and allowing the autobiographer to "take it as it was," in other words, to accept it. Theme and style are equivalent.

Thus, the resolution implied in the plot of the autobiography (with its emphasis on the autobiographical hero's acceptance of self-determination) is facilitated by the resolution implicit in the autobiographer's cathartic act of narrating his life story. The process of writing is a final return to and acceptance of the community of Harlem through a return to and acceptance of the past. At the moment of writing, Brown frees himself once again from psychological imprisonment by refusing to run from the past; instead, he imposes a pattern (form) upon its chaos. Precisely because writing becomes for Brown, as it was for Richard Wright, the ultimate escape route from slavery, and as it was for Eldridge Cleaver and Horace Cayton, the ultimate means to identity, to understand the way in which he patterns his experience is to understand how he achieves his radical breakthrough to identity.

Stylistically, Brown recreates an environment that represents in language the environment of Harlem, thus informing his life narrative with an immediacy that resurrects the qualitative reality of the past. As I have noted earlier, the first scene establishes the whole fabric of relationships in the community, immediately introducing its destructive and violent nature. From the first scene until the last scene with Reno, the terrible is omnipresent: loss, disappointment, violence, death. It is a way of life characterized by pervasive pain; it is a way of life whose Sundays are blood and vomit and people going to church, a way of life inherently ironic because it is filled with sharp juxtapositions and contradictions. This ironic world is imaginatively evoked by means of Brown's carefully controlled point of view, which maintains these juxtapositions in the description of scenes such as the Sunday morning vignette, in the description of characters like Mrs. Ganey who visits the injured boy's bedside, and in the description of attitudes. Brown, for example, concludes an early section in which he describes a family visit to Mrs. Rogers' church with this comment: "Maybe Dad was right when he said that Mrs. Rogers was just robbing people in the name of the Lord. Anyway, I felt pretty good about her not getting my nickel" (27). Apparent religiosity is actual thievery. There is irony enough in the reality of Mrs. Rogers' activities; there is more in the introduction to the next section, which begins: "Even though Dad didn't care for preachers, and churches, he had a lot of religion in his own way. Most of the time, his religion didn't show. But on Saturday nights, those who didn't see it heard it" (27). Real religion is in the bottle.

This painful, ironic existence is an essentially repetitious one, a quality Brown captures through the constant repetition of themes and key phrases. The words "run" and "I ran" appear over and over as Brown attempts to escape; they are the first words of chapters one and sixteen; and they are interspersed within each chapter as Brown runs from the police, from Harlem, to Harlem. There are the recurrent patterns involving the fates of his friends: Jackie and Sugar end up on the street "tricking"; Dunny and Kid die from overdoses; Jim Goldie is shot; Butch falls off a roof; Reno and Pimp go to jail; Brown himself keeps appearing before judges, keeps returning to or from reform school; his father keeps beating him; his mother keeps crying. His verbal model captures the cyclic nature of existence in Harlem. Moreover, the loose structural assemblage of incidents, which organize loosely around a plot line but not a strictly chronological one, emphasizes the repetitiousness. Often scenes that follow one another associate by (repeat) tone or theme: the opening associates a personal moment of violence with a community riot; the theme of religion and the ironic tone link the sections describing Mrs. Rogers' and his father's religious practices; later the chapter on Saturday nights describes two separate memorable Saturday night experiences that associate by the narrator's remembrance of Saturday nights in general. Constant repetition produces an imaginative structure through which the reader experiences emotionally rather than intellectually the horror of life and the difficulty of escaping the oppressive forces of an inherently repetitious existence.

The very power, strength, and effect of Brown's narrative lie also in his choices of language and diction. He recreates the reality of the life he lived and does so effectively by restricting himself to its language and speech idioms. There is a vocabulary of the streets that is a direct manifestation of street life. Brown's youth is spent learning this vocabulary. Often throughout the narrative, Brown introduces a word whose meaning he does not know: the next series of events relate his assumption of knowledge. Such terms as "catting," "hookie," "baby," "the Murphy"—all these words are not merely spoken or written words: they are his way of life.

The stylistic qualities accumulate to invest the life of Harlem with a concreteness and immediacy central to Brown's narrative intent. His goal is not intense introspection, which is not to imply that Brown is not self-conscious; his whole pain of dislocation and his need to tell about it are results of a nagging self-consciousness. He does not, however, narrate the inner landscape of his consciousness but focuses on the outer landscape of his life, on events in and out of Harlem that affect him. There are analytical moments but analytical of Harlem in general rather than of his own inner feelings. His inner landscape is revealed as it is externalized through his actions and through his conversations with others.

III

Brown's style of narration—the immediacy of the experience successfully captured through redundant but loose patterning, omnipresent horror and pain, an ironic tone, the intensely colloquial language itself, and the lack of introspection—is the technique of the blues singer, and his autobiography is itself a blueslike song. The blues is a peculiar response to the vicissitudes of life emanating from the black American experience, and thus, like the slave narrative, is wholly a black form. It is a form of individualized expression characterized basically by a repeated second line, a loose associative structure, colloquial language, irony, and painful lament. Without presuming to imply a one-to-one relationship between the blues and Brown's literary work, a relationship impossible because of the differing mediums of expression, I will suggest that there are similarities in purpose as well as technique, which enrich Brown's autobiographical achievement and further our appreciation of it to the extent that they are identified.

Certain qualities characteristic of the blues have already been identified as qualities of the slave narrative. In the act of writing, the slave narrator again liberated himself, now from psychological imprisonment in an oppressive past, by giving distance to his past through the imposition of artistic form. Through the use of such techniques as humor and irony, the narrator gained control over his memories and thereby transcended them. Their presence in *Black Boy* has been identified and explored by Ellison in his essay "Richard Wright's Blues":

Along with the themes, equivalent descriptions of milieu and the perspectives to be found in Joyce, Nehru, Dostoievsky, George Moore and Rousseau,

> *Black Boy* is filled with blues—tempered echoes of rail-
> road trains, the names of Southern towns and cities,
> estrangements, fights and flights, deaths and disap-
> pointments, charged with physical and spiritual hun-
> gers and pain. And like a blues sung by such an artist as
> Bessie Smith, its lyrical prose evokes the paradoxical,
> almost surreal image of a black boy singing lustily as he
> probes his own grievous wound.

And Ellison's own invisible man sings the blues of his invisibility. The prologue introduces the blues theme that weaves
throughout the novel when the protagonist declares:

> I play the invisible music of my isolation. The last
> statement doesn't seem just right, does it? But it is; you
> hear this music simply because music is heard and
> seldom seen, except by musicians. Could this compul-
> sion to put invisibility down in black and white be thus
> an urge to make music of invisibility? (11)

In the background, a record by Louis Armstrong asks,
"What did I do to be so black and blue?" which the protagonist rewords to introduce his narrative of his own experience, "But what did *I* do to be so blue?" (12). The
chapters that follow become the song of the "I" singing its
blues of invisibility, a song characterized by the repetition of
the same motif, the same line, as the protagonist suffers
constant reversals and disappointments. The singing itself
provides the "I" with a means to transcend the pains of that
experience and thus decide to return above ground to the
social roles of society: the febrile quality of the prologue
gives way to the qualified affirmation of the epilogue.
Through the act of singing his blues, the protagonist comes
to affirm as well as denounce, to love as well as hate. In this

way, he has transformed the liabilities of his identity into assets, the knowledge of reality into affirmation despite that knowledge and, in fact, based on it: "Life is to be lived, not controlled; and humanity is won by continuing to play in face of certain defeat" (499).

The blues singer is any individual who, needing desperately to verbalize the pain, the joy, the anger, of his daily life, makes of his experiences a lyric. This autobiographical quality distinguishes it from the ballad and the spiritual. Spirituals were originally meant for group singing and were religious in nature; ballads, in turn, told of some event or of a hero, for example, Joe Louis. The blues, on the other hand, is sung by the individual whose experiences they describe. In his history, *The Story of the Blues,* Paul Oliver explains that

> through the blues a man could sing about himself as he did in the fields; he could be his own hero. He could brag a little, he could make up a story about himself, he could wish himself into a situation—leaving home for better conditions or where there were no responsibilities. Or he could tell of the unhappiness of yesterday and work it out of his system. The blues was a way of singing and playing; it was a kind of song, and as always, it was a state of mind.[3]

Finally, the blues distinguishes itself from jazz, a derivative musical form similar in many ways, in its lack of introspection: jazz is a more introspective, more personal, less traditional, and therefore, a less representative experience.[4] In contrast, the bluesman, while singing of his own experience, gives expression to the experience of every man and, in this way, becomes a representative figure. As Charles Kiel observes in his study, *Urban Blues:* "For many

Negroes, life is one long sacrificial ritual. The blues artist, in telling his story, crystallizes and synthesizes not only his own experience but the experience of his listeners."[5]

The repetition of self-destruction in *Manchild* is the repetition of the ritual of self-sacrifice in Harlem. Brown, as a literary bluesman, sings of his own past and, in singing of that past, sings the blues of his peers in the Harlem community:

> I want to talk about the first Northern urban generation of Negroes. I want to talk about the experiences of a misplaced generation, of a misplaced people in an extremely complex, confused society. This is a story of their searching, their dreams, their sorrows, their small and futile rebellions, and their endless battle to establish their own place in America's greatest metropolis —and in America itself. (7)

He becomes the representative spokesman for his community, for, as one of them, he has shared the common experience of the group. But whereas the true bluesman, for the most part, sings for others indirectly by singing of himself, Brown also sings directly of their experiences when he tells of the fates of Jackie, Sugar, Tony, Pimp, and others. This fullness is a result of the length of the autobiography; it is actually a compendium of hundreds of blues songs.

Yet the fates of these others are integral to Brown's own journey to freedom. It is something of a miracle that he survives the self-destructive fate of so many of his peers, especially since he describes no overwhelming experience, such as that of Malcolm X, that saves him from that other fate. Perhaps his successful escape from destruction is a function of the failure of others in his peer group. In an oblique way, these others represent his other selves, the foils or masks, by means of which he can better see himself. They define the possibilities that he finally rejects but can reject only insofar as he sees their destructive reality. Their fates are involved in his fate; their pains and frustrations are really his own painful blues. And those blues must be sung.

A blues lyric puts forth a problem for which the act of singing becomes an antidote. In this sense, the blues, as Paul Oliver argues, are "basically accommodative" in that they offer release from pain by providing a catharsis through the act of singing: "The blues singer didn't reason himself into another state of mind, he sang himself into it."[6] They are, in effect, a means of psychoanalysis, a means to conquer the pains of living by retelling past experience until the singer understands it—until, that is, it takes on shape. The singing of the blues is thus essentially a ritual act through which the material of an individual's life is transformed into artistic form. According to Gene Bluestein, "the blues is not the 'power of positive thinking' but a transformation of catastrophe through the agency of art."[7] In singing or writing about past experience, the artist gives it distance and a context and, in this way, masters it and frees himself from the oppression of its emotional stress. Freedom is realized by means of an artistic control over experience, which results in the personal mastery and acceptance of that experience and thus of the self.

Brown's control over his material is more sophisticated than that of the blues singer in general. His structure and point of view are more complex. Nevertheless, by imposing form on the chaos of his life through writing an autobiography, by finding in this form itself adequate identity and freedom, Brown is the essential bluesman, finally freeing himself from subjection to the past. By accepting the past, he accepts responsibility for his own fate: this is the catharsis his blues lyric provides. Kiel contends that the central problem for the bluesman and for the black American in general is "not so much to discover or create a new identity as, first, to accept an identity that is already available and, second, to transform into working assets whatever crippling liabilities may be associated with that identity."[8] Brown as a literary blues singer comes to a fuller acceptance of himself by keeping the painful and beautiful memories alive within his soul, thus turning what seemed liabilities into assets. The central asset of such past experience involked becomes the recognition of self-control over one's fate, the final recognition of the plot, the recognition of the artist who controls his material.

Kiel further contends that "the blues man's self-acceptance sustains him in the crisis of maturity."[9] Brown's crisis can only be hypothesized from the implications in the text. The past weighs heavily upon his consciousness, urging him to recreate it, but for reasons not completely clear. There is the possibility that he suffers some indefinable guilt resulting not so much from a personal wrongdoing as from a social predicament in which the mere fact of survival is itself guilt inducing. When his friend Butch falls off a roof and dies, he visits Butch's mother who says to him, "Why, Sonny Boy, didn't you start using the damn dope too? Why did my Butch have to use that damn dope and go and kill himself? . . . Sonny Boy, why didn't you?' " (213). Brown knows only too well that what she really means is "Why aren't you dead too?" Perhaps to expiate this guilt, Brown sings these blues. Or there is the possibility that Brown needs to control his anger—an anger that continually controls him—through the artistic control of his past. The act of writing becomes the resolution which reassures Brown that man does control his own life, that he chooses to be what he becomes. This resolution relieves the guilt and controls the anger.

The act of writing also forces him once again to stop running away and to return to Harlem, in the end not only accepting but reaffirming his communal legacy. In this way, the nature of Brown's resolution bears an affinity to the jazz aesthetic as well as that of the blues. The jazz ensemble in performance enacts a musical dialogue between the group as a whole and the individual instrumentalist. The individual, in his drive for self-assertion, has his solo moments but is inevitably recalled to the group in which he functions and against which he defines himself. His freedom is the freedom to assert himself within the limits imposed on him by group membership. As Ellison writes in *Shadow and Act*:

> True jazz is an art of individual assertion within and against the group. Each true jazz moment . . . springs from a contest in which each artist challenges all the rest; each solo flight, or improvisation, represents . . . a definition of his identity: as individual, as member of a collectivity and as a link in the chain of tradition.[10]

Thus, each jazz performance is a process of accommodation between the individual and society. Bluestein writes:

> Jazz values improvisation, personal vision, an assault on the conventional modes of musical expression, but it will not allow the individual to forget what he owes to traditions—not the tradition of a great man, but the legacy shaped by a whole people.[11]

The individual is free to assert himself only if he recognizes the limitations imposed upon him by group membership.

This dialogue between the individual and the group is central to the text of *Manchild:* within the loose plot structure, Brown springs away from the group only to return and accept his communal identity. It is also central to the style: Brown flees from Harlem again only to return to reaffirm his communal legacy and finally to transcend it through the act of artistic catharsis. Brown can again pursue his own individual vision precisely because he has returned to Harlem to make his peace, even if only a temporary peace, for there is always the threat that the peace will pass, the past will break through again. Be that as it may, the fact is that *both* the final accommodation of the black self to his society and the radical breakthrough to personal freedom (an acceptance of self-determination within limitations) are achieved through the act of writing autobiography.

Notes

[1]Claude Brown, *Manchild in the Promised Land,* p. 8. Further citations will appear in the text.

[2]Ralph Ellison, "Richard Wright's Blues," *Shadow and Act,* p. 79.

[3]Paul Oliver, *The Story of the Blues,* p. 29.

[4]Dr. Wilbert C. Jordan, an authority on black music, suggested these distinctions between jazz and the blues and proved an invaluable source of information.

[5]Charles Keil, *Urban Blues,* p. 161.

[6]Oliver, *Story,* p. 29.

[7]Gene Bluestein, "The Blues as a Literary Theme," p. 609.

[8]Keil, *Urban Blues,* p. 15.

[9]Ibid., p. 201.

[10]Ralph Ellison, "The Charlie Christian Story," *Shadow and Act,* p. 234.

[11]Bluestein, "The Blues," p. 613.

BIBLIOGRAPHY

Black American autobiographies discussed in detail:

Angelou, Maya. *I Know Why the Caged Bird Sings.* New York: Random House, 1969.

Brown, Claude. *Manchild in the Promised Land.* New York: Macmillan Co., 1965.

Brown, William Wells. *Narrative of the Life of William W. Brown, A Fugitive Slave: Written by Himself.* Boston: Anti-Slavery Office, 1847.

Cayton, Horace. *Long Old Road.* New York: Trident Press, 1965.

Cleaver, Eldridge. *Soul On Ice.* New York: McGraw-Hill, 1968.

Hughes, Langston. *The Big Sea.* New York: Alfred A. Knopf, 1940.

Malcolm X. *The Autobiography of Malcolm X.* New York: Grove Press, 1965.

Washington, Booker T. *Up From Slavery.* Garden City, New York: Doubleday & Co., Inc., 1901.

Wright, Richard. *Black Boy.* New York: Harper & Row, 1945.

Other black American autobiographies mentioned in text:

Bailey, Pearl. *The Raw Pearl.* New York: Harcourt, Brace & World, 1968.

Craft, William. *Running a Thousand Miles for Freedom: or the Escape of William and Ellen Craft.* London: W. Tweedie, 1860.

Douglass, Frederick. *My Bondage and My Freedom, Part I—Life as a Slave, Part II—Life as a Freeman.* New York: Miller, Orton & Mulligan, 1855.

DuBois, W. E. B. *Dusk of Dawn*. New York: Harcourt, Brace and Co., 1940.

Gibson, Althea. *I Always Wanted to Be Somebody*. Edited by Ed Fitzgerald. New York: Harper Bros., 1958.

Green, Ely. *Ely*. New York: Seabury Press, 1966.

Handy, W.C. *Father of the Blues*. New York: The Macmillan Co., 1941.

Horne, Lena, and Schickel, Richard. *Lena*. Garden City, New York: Doubleday, 1965.

Hughes, Langston. *I Wonder as I Wander: An Autobiographical Sketch*. New York: Rinehart, 1956.

Jackson, George. *Soledad Brother: The Prison Letters of George Jackson*. New York: Coward-McCann, 1970.

Jackson, Mahalia. *Movin' On Up*. New York: Hawthorn Books, 1966.

Jones, LeRoi. *Home*. New York: Morrow, 1966.

Lane, Lunsford. *The Narrative of Lunsford Lane, Formerly of Raleigh, North Carolina*. Boston: Published by Himself, 1842.

Louis, Joe. *The Joe Louis Story*. New York: Grosset & Dunlop, 1953.

McKay, Claude. *A Long Way from Home*. New York: Lee Furman, Inc., 1937.

Mays, Willie. *Born to Play Ball: My Life In and Out of Baseball*. New York: Dutton, 1966.

Moore, Archie. *The Archie Moore Story*. New York: McGraw-Hill, 1960.

Northup, Solomon. *Twelve Years a Slave: Narrative of Solomon Northup*. Auburn: Derby & Miller, 1853.

Patterson, Floyd. *Victory Over Myself*. New York: Bernard Geis Associates, 1962.

Pickens, William. *Bursting Bonds*. Boston: The Jordan and More Press, 1923.

Powell, Lt. William J. *Black Wings*. Los Angeles: Ivan Deach, Jr., Publisher, 1934.

Redding, J. Saunders. *No Day of Triumph*. New York: Harper & Bros., 1942.

Robinson, Jackie. *Breakthrough to the Big League*. New York: Harper & Row, 1965.

Taylor, William W. "Major". *The Fastest Bicycle Rider in the World*. Worcester, Massachusetts: Wormley Publishing Co., 1928.

Primary and Secondary Sources in Black American Literature

Baldwin, James. *Nobody Knows My Name: More Notes of a Native Son*. New York: Dial Press, 1961.

————. *Notes of a Native Son*. New York: Dial Press, 1963.

Barton, Rebecca Chalmers. *Witnesses for Freedom: Negro Americans in Autobiography*. New York: Harper and Row, 1948.

Bluestein, Gene. "The Blues as a Literary Theme." *The Massachusetts Review* 8 (1967): 593-617.

Bone, Robert A. *The Negro Novel in America*. New Haven: Yale University Press, 1958.

Bontemps, Arna, ed. *Great Slave Narratives*. Boston: Beacon Press, 1969.

Brown, Sterling A., Davis, Arthur P. and Lee, Ulysses. *The Negro Caravan: Writings by American Negroes*. New York: Dryden Press, 1941.

Charters, Samuel B. *The Poetry of the Blues*. New York: Oak Publications, 1963.

Clotman. Phyllis. "The Running Man as Metaphor in Contemporary Negro Literature." Ph.D. dissertation, Case Western Reserve University, 1969.

Davis, Ossie. "On Malcolm X." *The Autobiography of Malcolm X*. New York: Grove Press, 1966.

DuBois, W.E.B. *The Souls of Black Folk: Essays and Sketches*. Chicago: McClurg, 1903.

Ellison, Ralph. *Invisible Man*. New York: Random House, 1952.

————. *Shadow and Act*. New York: Random House, 1964.

Farrison, William Edward. *William Wells Brown: Author and Reformer*. Chicago: University of Chicago Press, 1969.

Franklin, John Hope, ed. *Three Negro Classics*. New York: Avon Books, 1965.

Glickberg, Charles I. "Negro Fiction in America." *South Atlantic Quarterly* 45 (October 1946): 482.

Grier, William H., and Cobbs, Price M. *Black Rage.* New York: Basic Books, 1968.

Hill, Herbert, ed. *Anger and Beyond: The Negro Writer in the United States.* New York: Harper and Row, 1966.

Jackson, Margaret Young. "An Investigation of Biographies and Autobiographies of American Slaves Published Between 1840 and 1860." Ph.D. dissertation, Cornell University, 1954.

Keil, Charles. *Urban Blues.* Chicago: University of Chicago Press, 1966.

Lester, Julius. *Look Out, Whitey! Black Power's Gon' Get Your Mama!* New York: Dial Press, 1968.

Litwack, Leon F. *North of Slavery: The Negro in the Free States, 1790-1860.* Chicago: University of Chicago Press, 1961.

Margolies, Edward. *Native Sons: A Critical Study of Twentieth-Century Negro American Authors.* Philadelphia: J.B. Lippincott, 1968.

Meier, August, and Rudwick, Elliott M. *From Plantation to Ghetto.* New York: Hill & Wang, 1966.

Nichols, Charles H. *Many Thousand Gone: The Ex-Slaves' Account of Their Bondage and Freedom.* Leiden, Netherlands: E.J. Brill, 1963.

Ohman, Carol. "The Autobiography of Malcolm X: A Revolutionary use of the Franklin Tradition." *American Quarterly* 22 (Summer 1970): 131-149.

Oliver, Paul. *The Story of the Blues.* Philadelphia: Chilton Book Co., 1969.

Osofsky, Gilbert, ed. *Puttin' on Ole Massa: The Slave Narratives of Henry Bibb, William Wells Brown, and Solomon Northup.* New York: Harper & Row, 1969.

Reilly, John. Afterword to *Native Son* by Richard Wright. New York: Harper and Row, 1966.

Scott, Emmett J., and Stowe, Lyman Beecher. *Booker T. Washington: Builder of a Civilization.* Garden City, New York: Doubleday, Page & Co., 1917.

Scott, Nathan A., Jr. "The Dark and Haunted Tower of Richard Wright." In Gibson, Donald B., ed. *Five Black Writers.* New York: New York University Press, 1970, 12-25.

Toomer, Jean. *Cane.* New York: Boni and Liveright, 1923.

Webb, Constance. *Richard Wright: A Biography.* New York: G.P. Putnam's Sons, 1968.

Wright, Richard. *Native Son.* New York: Harper & Row, 1940.

General Literary Criticism

Axthelm, Peter M. *The Modern Confessional Novel.* New Haven: Yale University Press, 1967.

Booth, Wayne. *The Rhetoric of Fiction.* Chicago: University of Chicago Press, 1961.

Campbell, Joseph. *The Hero with a Thousand Faces.* New York: Pantheon Books, 1949.

Galloway, David D. *The Absurd Hero in American Fiction.* Austin: University of Texas Press, 1966.

Hassan, Ihab. *Radical Innocence: Studies in the Contemporary American Novel.* Princeton: Princeton University Press, 1961.

Kellogg, Robert, and Scholes, Robert. *The Nature of Narrative.* New York: Oxford University Press, 1966.

Kermode, Frank. *The Sense of an Ending: Studies in the Theory of Fiction.* New York: Oxford University Press. 1967.

Klein, Marcus. *After Alienation: American Novels in Mid-century.* Cleveland: World Publishing Co., 1964.

Lewis, R.W.B. *The Picaresque Saint: Representative Figures in Contemporary Fiction.* London: Victor Gollancz, 1960.

Minter, David L. *The Interpreted Design as a Structural Principle in American Prose.* New Haven: Yale University Press, 1969.

Olney, James. *Metaphors of Self.* Princeton: Princeton University Press, 1972.

Pascal, Roy. *Design and Truth in Autobiography.* Cambridge: Harvard University Press, 1960.

Poirier, Richard. *A World Elsewhere: The Place of Style in American Literature.* New York: Oxford University Press, 1966.

Rubin, Louis D., Jr. *The Teller of the Tale*. Seattle: Washington University Press, 1967.

Sayre, Robert. *The Examined Self*. Princeton: Princeton University Press, 1964.

Shea, Daniel B., Jr. *Spiritual Autobiography in Early America*. Princeton: Princeton University Press, 1968.

Stevick, Philip. *The Theory of the Novel*. New York: The Free Press, 1967.

Walcutt, Charles Child. *Man's Changing Masks: Modes and Methods of Characterization in Fiction*. Minneapolis: University of Minnesota Press, 1966.

Weinberg, Helen. *The New Novel in America: the Kafkan Mode in Contemporary Fiction*. Ithaca: Cornell University Press, 1970.

INDEX